Paul B. Kidd's

AMAZING FISHING TALES

HarperCollinsPublishers

Cover Illustration: Brendan Akhurst
Internal Illustrations: Brendan Akhurst

HarperCollins*Publishers*

First published in Australia in 1997
by HarperCollins*Publishers* Pty Limited
ACN 009 913 517
A member of HarperCollins*Publishers* (Australia) Pty Limited Group
http://www.harpercollins.com.au

HarperCollins*Publishers*
25 Ryde Road, Pymble, Sydney NSW 2073, Australia
31 View Road, Glenfield, Auckland 10, New Zealand
77–85 Fulham Palace Road, London W6 8JB, United Kingdom
Hazelton Lanes, 55 Avenue Road, Suite 2900, Toronto, Ontario M5R 3L2
and 1995 Markham Road, Scarborough, Ontario M1B 5M8, Canada
10 East 53rd Street, New York NY 10032, USA

National Library of Australia Cataloguing-in-Publication data:

Kidd, Paul B. (Paul Benjamin), 1945-.
Paul B. Kidd's amazing fishing tales.
ISBN 0 7322 5964 9

1. Fishing - Australia - Anecdotes. 2. Fishing - Australia - Humour.
I. Title. II. Title: Amazing fishing tales.

799.10207.
Printed in Australia by Griffin Press on 80gsm Econoprint.

5 4 3 2 1
01 00 99 98 97

Dedication

To Alan Morris, the genius who co-founded Mojo, the cleverest bloke I know and a wonderful friend. And to the person I love more than anything in the whole wide world, my 19-year-old budding art director son, Benny.

Acknowledgments

Thanks to my good friend Charles Wooley for the foreword; Brendan Akhurst for his wonderful drawings; Victoria Conant for editorial assistance; Benny Kidd for all the editorial running around; and all the colourful characters, both real and fictitious, dead and alive, sober or flyblown, without whose assistance this book wouldn't have been possible.

Contents

Foreword, by Charles Wooley ix

The Deep Sea Contract 1

Eighteen Marlin . . . In One Day 9

Gaffer Bourke 14

Heli-fishing to Adventure 22

The Hunt Comes Up Trump 30

The Loaded Croc 36

Lureitis . . . Fishing's Deadliest Disease 44

The Fish Hit Parade — Tuna Up in the Key of Sea 51

Thirsty Bert 57

My Hero — Bob Dyer 63

The Topless Shark 67

A Grand Tale 74

The Revenge of the Giant Mullet 80

Tacklin' Tassie's Tuna 85

'Women and Children First? Not Always.' 93

Moreton and Luna Park 100

Crocodile Boots 104

A Tall Tale of Tagged Trout 110

The Sharks of Sugartown 117

The Duck, the Chemist and Billy the Pig 125

Love on the Rocks 133
Things that Float 138
They'll Eat Anything 142
Sir Adrian's Record 148
The Fishermen Aren't Biting 153
The Big Bad Bull Shark 157
SeaDuced by a Reel Screamer 161
Skidmarks and the Judge 165
Mind-bending Marlin 171
The Last of the Shark Hunters 175
The Day of the Great White Death 179
The Bottle Shop Bargain 183
Flies, Like Martinis, Should be Dry 187
The Deaf Snapper 193
The Darker Side of Fishing Knives 200
Mugged in Paradise 205
The Shark Arm Murder 210
Fangs for the Memories 214
Fishing's Urban Myths 218
Those Magnificently Mad Makos 225
Toady's Revenge 232

Foreword

When I first met Paul B. Kidd he was on the rocks. A rock shelf, to be exact, pounded by huge Pacific rollers. We were shooting a story about the large number of people who are swept to their death each year while rock fishing. That's *60 Minutes* for you; we only get to go fishing if someone dies.

Paul did his best to drown us both but we ended up with only a thorough soaking and the beginnings of what I am sure will be a lifelong friendship.

Paul is one of the great characters of Australian fishing though, come to think of it, we didn't catch a fish that day. Or any other day for that matter. Indeed, since then we have done all our fishing at lunch, or in the pub. I'm sure that in between talking and writing about fishing he must occasionally do some. But look, any dill can throw a line! Spinning the yarn is the trick, hooking the audience and holding them. That's what Paul does best. He's a spellbinder. Sometimes I come away from our encounters, my sides aching and my face hurting from laughing so much. When he's on a roll you just hang onto your seat and hope to stay dry.

Read a chapter such as 'Toady's Revenge' and you will know exactly what I mean. Paul has the happy knack of writing it exactly the way he tells it. 'Savage little bastards that we were . . . We stabbed them, threw them under cars . . . teed off using them as golf balls . . .'

Or Paul the not so intrepid in 'Heli-fishing to Adventure' in deepest creepy-crawly infested far north Queensland. 'And then we were there, dumped straight into knee-high undergrowth. If Elle Macpherson was 100 metres away in the nude beckoning to me and the only thing between us was knee-high undergrowth, I'd never get to see that magnificent body up close.'

Paul writes as he speaks and part of the charm of this book is that the Editor has been sensible enough not to remove his rough edges. At a time when so much fishing writing is boringly over-technical or mere bland pap, Paul's funny, abrasive style of writing rubs us up the right way.

As his mate I am often asked by his readers, 'Are those stories really true?' Despite our friendship I always try to answer as honestly as I can; that I am sure they are true to the best of Paul's recollection and within the limitations of his self-control as a gifted storyteller.

The inquiring reader is usually still laughing too much to hear my two qualifications: that Paul B. is memorably forgetful, and that this is probably a result of his total lack of self-control.

Charles Wooley
October 1997

The Deep Sea Contract

I have fished with many famous and notorious people over the years and of them all I loved Theo the Boss the most. As sinister as he seemed to the rest of the world, Theo was always good to me, and he was my friend. Although I have changed some of the names and the circumstances are slightly varied, this is a true story.

I will never forget that day as long as I live. We were fishing off Sydney for sharks on Theo the Boss's 56-foot game-fishing boat *Saint Theodore*. But believe me, Theo was no saint. Theo was a very heavy member of organised crime and had plenty of politicians and cops in Sydney in his pocket. Theo was 'The Man'.

And only now that Theo is pushing up daisies can I tell this story.

Through the '60s and '70s, Theo the Boss ran Sydney's biggest illegal casino, the Nugget Club, with an iron fist. Collecting bad debts and rubbing shoulders with racketeers, standover men and hired killers was all in a night's work.

And the Boss had them all terrified. He was a proper gangster, straight out of a '30s movie. If there was an Edward G. Robinson look-alike competition, Theo the Boss would have run first, third and ninth.

A short, stocky Greek with a patent leather haircut and pencil-thin moustache, Theo dressed appropriately in handmade double-breasted Raymond Peraggio suits, bright ties and spit-polished two-tone Meller's shoes. He wore a diamond the size of a duck egg on the small finger of his left hand, smoked huge Cuban cigars and drank only the finest Scotch whisky.

The Boss was chauffeur-driven around town by his ever-present henchman, Gringo, in a huge black Mark V four-door Lincoln

HEY BOSS!
THERE'S A BOAT
DOIN' NUTHIN'
BUT FISHIN'!!
GET READY...
GET SETTY...
OK FISH
~SO WHAT'S
IT TO BE?
LEFTY
DUTCH
WILLY

Continental Town Car with pitch-black windows. 'The Mafia staff car', the boys called it.

Gringo carried the biggest gun I have ever seen in my life, and if anyone suspicious came within cooee of the Boss he would produce it and, if need be, use it.

Being offside with the Boss was not a good place to be. But if you were his friend, he was the best bloke in the world and couldn't do enough for you. Money was no object, and he would spray his clan with the best of everything. The Boss was a beaut bloke and I crewed for him on *Saint Theodore* and I was his friend.

The Boss's two great passions were swearing and fishing — in that order. And he didn't give a shit who he dropped the magic word in front of. In a twenty-word sentence, eighteen of them would be swearwords. And with the Boss's thick accent and sinister delivery, it was hilarious to hear him unleash a gobful on someone and reduce them to a gibbering mess. Mind you, none of us ever laughed to his face.

Whenever he could, the Boss would escape the gawdy decor and the hustle and bustle of the Nugget Club and go fishing on his magnificent *Saint Theodore*, which was the apple of his eye.

She had every possible extra, and the Boss kept her like a new pin. We even had to take our shoes off before we walked inside. To do anything wrong on *Saint Theodore* was putting your life in very grave danger.

'Paul B., you fuckin' bastard. You like fuckin' fishin' on my bloody fuckin' beauty boat?' Theo would always ask me as he sat back in his giant leather lounge chair. He would be chewing on a mammoth Monte Cristo and sucking on a vase of 20-year-old Chivas Regal as we headed out to the fishing grounds many miles off the Sydney coastline at around 7am.

'Absolutely, Theo,' I would always reply. 'Fishing on the best boat in the country with you is always fun. There's certainly never a dull moment.' And it was the truth.

Gringo would always analyse what I had said, his dull brain trying to figure out if I was taking the piss out of the Boss or not, in case he had to tug my coat. He never had to.

Cutting into the nicotine and alcohol at dawn was perfectly normal for Theo. After all, he'd been up all night running his gambling house, and counting the money into the small hours of the morning; to Theo and his henchman, it was just like going to the pub at five o'clock after a hard day's work.

Curiously, Theo the Boss didn't do much big game fishing himself, preferring to handline for snapper — or snappers, as he called them. So every Sunday we would fish for 'snappers' and every other Sunday we would fish the point-scoring competition for marlin, tuna and sharks for the Sydney Game Fishing Club. And we did extremely well.

Our crew consisted of the legendary Watsons Bay boatman, Jack Farrell, the Boss's son Nicky, Gringo and myself. Jack was in his early seventies and had gaffed countless world records for most of the big names in game fishing. There wasn't much old Jack didn't know about bluewater fishing.

The Boss and Jack got on like a house on fire. They were about the same age, and the Boss didn't have to put on any of that gangster bullshit with Jack. They would just sit and talk about fishing over a fine old Scotch. Jack wasn't in the least bit interested in what the Boss did for a quid; he seemed totally oblivious to the fact that he was the fishing master for the heaviest mobster in Sydney, if not Australia.

Theo's son Nicky was a terrific bloke in his early thirties who had no interest whatever in following in the family tradition and was content to run his small law practice, which specialised in conveyancing.

Nicky loved anything to do with boats and fishing, and drove the boat while Jack and I looked after the gear and rigged the baits. We took it in turns to catch the marlin, sharks and tuna, and the Boss didn't care if he caught a game fish or not. He much preferred handlining for the 'snappers'.

The Boss often entertained characters that we had only seen photos of and read about in the papers, and they would huddle and whisper in the saloon of the boat with the door closed while drinking whisky amid an expensive fog of blue cigar smoke.

'Don't you take any notice of what you see or hear in there, young

fella,' wise old Jack would whisper to me as we rigged the baits and set the lines. 'Fishermen live a lot longer than gangsters.'

Gringo always came along for the ride. He looked out of place at sea with his fedora hat sloped over his eyes and the huge cannon bulging under his jacket, but it was his job to see that the Boss came to no harm, no matter where he was.

This day we were berleying and drifting the Twelve Mile Reef with big surface baits, looking for sharks. It was mid-August, and the seas were as flat as a night-carter's hat. August is mako shark time, and they are the meanest, most unpredictable things that swim. They twist and turn in the gaff ropes and often jump into the boat with their jaws snapping at anything that gets in their way. They are often referred to as 'blue dynamite with a short fuse'.

We hadn't been drifting long when a mako of about 250 pounds took a bait right at the back of the boat and I took the strike. It gave me a good fight for an hour or so, leaping all over the ocean, before Jack finally gaffed it and secured it to the side of the boat.

The next strike was another mako of around 300 pounds, which Nicky took, and after another hard fight of half an hour or so, it too was captured and tied off to a bollard.

Then another mako swam right up to the back of the boat and tried to eat the berley pot. It was a big bastard and it had its mouth around the stainless steel chum pot and was trying to wrench it from the boat.

Jack ran inside and got the Australian record chart. 'How big do you reckon that fish is, Paul?' he asked, knowing that I had seen more than my share of big makos over the years.

'I reckon 600 pounds would stop it cold, Jack,' I said as I admired the great fish's magnificent shades of blue and its superb shape. It looked as if it could have been carved out of onyx. Dreading what was to come, I wondered if guided missiles had been designed using makos as the template.

I knew that I would probably be called upon to kill this beautiful eating machine soon, and I hated doing it. But back in those kill-anything-that-swims days of the '60s and '70s it was my job . . . and that was that.

'The Australian record for a mako on 20 pound line is just over 500 pounds, and this bloke is around 550 pounds,' Jack said as he threaded half a striped tuna onto a huge hook, attached it to a rod and reel fitted with 20 pound line and fed the bait down the big mako's throat. 'OK, let's get ourselves an Australian record that won't be beaten in a hurry.'

The Boss wasn't into catching sharks, so he sat on the flying bridge sipping on a Chivas, puffing away on a cigar and happily watching the activity and chatting with Gringo. He didn't give a damn for game fishing. Next week he would catch some 'snappers'.

Jack wound up the drag on the reel and sunk the hook, expecting the big fish to take off. But it didn't budge. It just stayed there, munching on the berley pot and swimming from one side of the boat to the other.

'Piss off, you bastard,' Jack yelled at the shark, but it didn't. It just hung around the back of the boat, offering no resistance at all. So I prodded it with the blunt end of a boat hook. That did the trick, and with one almighty swish of its tail — which nearly drenched us — it took off like a burning dog.

Jack leaned on the rod in an effort to fight the fish, and after about 200 metres of line had disappeared off the reel it seemed that he was winning. Then the line went slack. Jack wound as fast as he could, but he couldn't get fast to the fish again. We thought he had busted.

But no. 'The bloody thing's swimming back to the berley pot quicker than I can wind in the line,' Jack yelled in amazement. And then the mako materialised at the back of the boat, munching on the pot, and oblivious to the wire trace hanging out of its gob. It didn't know that it was hooked.

'Get the gaff,' yelled Jack. 'It's taken enough line off the reel to be considered a legal catch. Gaff it.'

'Bullshit,' I said. 'Are you crazy? Those things are mental enough at the gaff when they are exhausted after they've been fought for hours. Do you expect me to gaff one green?'

'Yes. So don't argue with me. Just do as you're told.'

I had no choice. That's the unwritten law of the ocean. The captain kicks the mate, the mate kicks the cabin boy, and the cabin boy kicks the cat. Like it or lump it, on a boat you do as you're told. I looked up at the Boss for a second opinion and maybe a bit of sympathy.

'Do as he bloody fuckin' says,' Theo the Boss growled, obviously unaware that in a minute I would be killed.

So I did as Jack commanded. I attached the end of the flying gaff rope to a bollard on the deck in the corner of the tuck, leaned over the back of the boat, placed the gaff head perfectly into the shark's shoulder just below the gills and pulled on the gaff pole and rope at the same time. It went straight in.

None of us were prepared for what happened next. The water erupted as if a depth charge had gone off just below the surface. And as if gaining momentum to leap into the boat and bite my head off for sticking that mammoth gaff into it, the shark plunged as deep as the length of the 14-foot gaff rope would allow and then shot through the surface, leapt the full length of the rope in mid-air above our heads and came crashing down onto the transom of the boat, snapping, blurting, grunting and biting at anything within snapping distance. Curiously, even though this was a moment of sheer terror, I can recall its breath. Yuk. It was vile.

Fortunately for us, it fell out of the boat and not into the cockpit, but as it did, it lifted the gaff rope over my head and behind me, pinning me in the corner of the boat between the bollard and the fish, which was still going berserk on the end of the gaff rope. I was copping rope burns all over my legs and back as the fish lunged and jumped, trying to throw the gaff.

Theo the Boss was far from impressed with what was happening to his pride and joy, and was even less impressed when the huge fish started breaking its teeth on the marlin board and smashing holes in the polished fibreglass hull with its tail. Finally he'd had enough.

'Look what that bloody fuckin' bastard's doing to my bloody beautiful boat! No bastard does that and gets away with it. Gringo, shoot that motherfucker,' he screamed.

Although he didn't know it, the Boss had probably just put out the world's first contract on a shark. And Gringo didn't have to be told twice. He produced the huge cannon from under his jacket and climbed down the flying bridge ladder, waving it in the air. As he hit the deck he aimed and took a shot at the shark as it propelled itself above the tuck of the boat.

I felt the bullet whistle past my ear as it missed the shark and landed in the water a hundred yards off the back of the boat. By this stage I had somehow managed to get the gaff rope over my head but I was bloodied and bruised from head to foot. Nicky had broken a finger trying to get a tail rope on the shark and now we had a totally pissed-off shark and a gun-totin' lunatic to contend with.

The Boss looked on at the mayhem below him and seemed to be enjoying it all. Just as Gringo was about to rattle off another shot, Jack called a halt to proceedings.

'Theo,' he called. 'You can't gaff a record fish with a .45 handgun. It will be disqualified. If we take that fish in with bullet holes in it there will be an uproar. Call Gringo off.'

The Boss listened to Jack and told Gringo to put the smoking gun away. Thank Christ for that. But we still had the shark to contend with. From the time I gaffed it to the time we finished tying it to the side of the boat was 45 minutes. We had been battered from one side of the boat to the other and we had the bruises and broken bones to prove it. Not to mention the near-death experience with a bullet.

The mako weighed 556 pounds. An Australian record at the time on 20 pound breaking-strain line.

Eighteen Marlin . . . In One Day

The mighty marlin . . . the most prized game fish in the ocean. To see one is a thrill, but to catch one is a dream far beyond most anglers' imagination. To catch 18 in a single day . . . astonishing! But it really did happen.

To most anglers, catching a marlin would be the angling feat of a lifetime, a thrill only surpassed by watching it swim away as it was set free to fight another day.

To anglers all over the world, marlin are the ultimate sportfish. However, the closest the average angler would ever get to one would be seeing it on TV or reading about it in fishing magazines or books such as this.

And even those anglers fortunate enough to be in a position to fish the places where marlin are most likely to be found . . . the deep waters far offshore . . . often spend years before they hook a marlin, let alone land it, and in lots of cases they never catch one at all.

Yes, to catch a marlin is a highlight in any angler's career. To catch and *release* a marlin is a *milestone* in an angler's career.

But to the marlin boat captains and crews who catch and release countless marlin day in and day out throughout the marlin season, there are various milestones and achievements that are far and beyond the average angler's imagination.

Such as one boat catching and releasing 18 marlin in a day! That's right, there's no need to adjust your set . . . 18 marlin in a single day's fishing . . . and every one of them was released to fight another day.

For the past ten years or so 50-year-old Captain Ross Hunter has chartered his magnificent 12-metre game-fishing boat *Broadbill* out of Botany Bay. He and his crew, son Glenn and Scott 'Big Bat'

Taunton (who are also both qualified sea captains), and their paying customers troll or berley and drift Sydney's prolific offshore waters for blue, black and striped marlin, yellowfin tuna and mako, blue, whaler and tiger sharks. And they catch plenty of them all.

But first and last, *Broadbill* is a marlin boat. The boys and their clients fish for sharks and tuna through the winter months when the marlin are scarce, but marlin is what this ship is all about. And *Broadbill*'s got the figures to prove it.

In a career of marlin fishing dating back to the early '80s, Ross Hunter's various boats have caught over 1000 marlin, of which 800 plus were taken in the past ten years while chartering on *Broadbill.*

And of all of those marlin, only ten or so were killed. The rest were released to be caught another day. The potential Zane Greys are informed the minute they set foot on *Broadbill* that marlin fishing is for the thrill and not the kill. Unless they come up dead, the fish are released.

'We don't kill any marlin, not even an angler's first fish,' Captain Ross tells his anglers. 'People don't kill marlin any more. In my opinion an angler who needs to kill a marlin for his ego hasn't quite made it as an angler.'

And that's that. There's even a sticker on *Broadbill*'s bulkhead which says: 'Real Men Don't Kill Marlin.' Gutsy stuff.

'Naturally enough, the day I got my first marlin was a day I'll never forget,' Ross recalls. 'It was certainly a milestone in my fishing career. And then there were the times when we caught two and then three in a day. But that was about the limit.

'Another milestone was a huge yellowfin tuna of 97 kilograms that we caught. It was the biggest I'd ever seen. Then in 1993 we caught the biggest blue marlin ever taken in New South Wales waters, a fish of 297 kilograms on 24 kilogram breaking-strain line.

'The bloke who caught it, Harvey Sainsbury, had never held a fishing rod before in his life and had never caught a fish of any description, let alone a huge marlin. Sadly the giant fish came up dead. We decided to bring it in and weigh it rather than leave it for the sharks.

'Coming into the 1996/97 marlin season, the best season we'd had was the one previous with a total of 78 marlin,' Ross explained. 'There had been record catches of marlin off Cairns, both inside and outside the Great Barrier Reef, toward the end of 1996 and, as the smaller marlin make the pilgrimage south each year, we knew that this season would be a bottler; but never in our wildest dreams did we imagine that it would turn out the way it did.

'Off Sydney we caught a few marlin in December, but in January they were thick. First we caught five in a day, then six in a day a week later, then nine . . . all in a single day. And what made it more exciting was that the majority of them were striped marlin of up to about 100 kilograms and they are real crackerjacks that jump all over the ocean and put on a dazzling aerial display. It was really exciting fishing.'

But the best was yet to come when Ross and the crew took *Broadbill* 300 kilometres north on their annual pilgrimage to Port Stephens to fish the Interclub Game Fishing Tournament and take out charters over an eight-week period.

'Last year at Port Stephens we caught 38 marlin,' Ross recalled, 'but this year they were everywhere. During the four-day tournament there were over 1000 marlin tagged and released by the 250 competing boats. We caught 23 marlin in the event and didn't run a place. That'll give you an idea of how many fish were caught.'

Author's note: 'Tagging' a marlin is done by inserting a tiny, stainless steel, non-retractable arrowhead into the marlin's shoulder. A piece of yellow plastic tubing about as thick as a piece of spaghetti is attached to the arrowhead. The tubing has a number on it that corresponds with the number on a card that is filled in by the angler, giving all of the details of the catch; estimated size, where caught, when, etc, and this card is recorded with Fisheries. If and when the fish is recaught, the tag number is looked up. The system gives scientists a more accurate idea of the movement of marlin all over the world, and of their growth rates.

Broadbill stayed on at Port Stephens after the tournament, taking out charters every day and catching marlin every day. They also chalked up a new record for the boat of 12 marlin in a day. Mind you, the marlin weren't huge — blacks and stripes of up to 125 kilograms — but they gave the customers a wonderful time, considering that most of them had never seen one before.

'A boat called *Calypso* had tagged 17 marlin in one day during the tournament. This was acknowledged as a record for New South Wales waters simply because no one had ever heard of that many marlin being taken in a single day by one boat before,' Ross said.

'No one could believe that it had been done, let alone that this new record could be broken. It was a truly extraordinary feat.

'This day we had chartered the boat to six real knockabout blokes. None of them had ever caught a marlin. None of them had ever seen a marlin. We left the dock at 7am and were trolling fish baits by 8am at the spot where we had caught most of our fish previously. Nothing. Not a scale. No surface activity. No bait patches on the sounder. No birds. Zilch.

'By one o'clock that afternoon I was trying to figure out which one of the six anglers had killed the Chinaman. Then I came across a current line in 20 fathoms off Little Island. The water had turned a deep blue, and the screen on the fishfinder blotched out indicating huge schools of slimy mackerel bait fish in the area. We had found 'em.

'Instantly we had a triple hook-up. One jumped off and we tagged and released a black and a striped marlin in the 40–60 kilogram range. We trolled north towards Broughton Island and the surface was just boiling with bait. There were fish everywhere.

'We had five double hook-ups and got the lot. By 6.30pm Scotty and Glenn counted 16 tag cards and it was only then that we realised we could break *Calypso*'s record. "Let's go for it", we yelled and went about our fishing with renewed enthusiasm. With daylight saving we figured we still had about two hours of fishing left.

'It wasn't until seven o'clock that we hooked another fish,' Ross recalled, 'and I nursed the boat gently and gave the angler every bit of assistance I could. It was pretty nerve-racking stuff.

'When we tagged it and equalled the record, everyone cheered, shook hands and yelled, and we went hunting for the record-breaker.

But we couldn't raise a fish. I decided to take a punt and steamed back to Little Island. As we put the baits in the water — the sun was going down now — we hooked up to a solid black marlin of around 70 kilograms, the biggest fish of the day.

'If I said I wasn't nervous, I'd be telling you a lie. I wanted that fish and the record that went with it desperately. Gently, gently the angler played it to the boat and we all breathed a huge sigh of relief when Scotty finally placed the tag in its shoulder and we cut it free.

'Drink? Did anyone say would I like a drink? Yup, we had a few that night and we deserved every one of 'em.

'Great boat, great crew, great blokes and the best day's fishing you could ever imagine. But I can't help wondering how long it will take for someone to break that record for New South Wales waters. When they do, I'll be the first bloke to buy 'em a drink.'

Gaffer Bourke

Every sport, including fishing, has its unsung heroes. Rodeos have the clowns, cross-country rallies have the navigators and fishing has the trace and gaff men and women, who carry out the thankless and extremely dangerous tasks. This story is about the greatest gaffer of them all and a tribute to gaffers and tracers everywhere.

In every critical situation there's a hero or a lunatic, or a heroic lunatic — just depends on how you look at it. It would be fair to say that the engineers in the Vietnam War, the brave men who went ahead of the troops and searched for booby-trapped tunnels, were real heroes, putting their lives on the line daily.

And during the American Civil War, the brave, yet naively foolish soldiers, some as young as twelve, would huddle together on their opposite sides the night before a battle and help each other sew large numbers on the backs of their tunics so that their bodies could be identified the following day when they would most certainly be killed, and their loved ones could then be notified of their heroic deaths.

On the other hand, it could be said that the Japanese Kamikaze (meaning divine wind) pilots of World War II were complete fools who flew their planes on suicide missions into the pride of the American navy to ensure themselves an easy ride into the next life.

Sorry, but even if you could convince me that Elle Macpherson, Demi Moore, Cindy Crawford and Marilyn Monroe were waiting for me on the other side with Dom Perignon poured, beluga caviar chilled and grapes peeled, I'm still not going to fly my plane into the side of a battleship about a mile long with all its guns blazing at me.

The old story goes that the Kamikaze instructor was informing the would-be pilots that they only had enough fuel to get out to the

American fleet. When they got there, they had to fly their planes into the biggest battleship they could find and kill themselves and as many Americans as they could for the glory of Japan.

He asked if there were any questions and a guy at the back called out: 'Are you serious? Are there any questions????'

God or no God, to my mind, that last lot were complete dills. I have a selection of ways I want to die, and believe me, flying a plane into a battleship isn't even in the first 25 000.

So there you have it, the three examples. Brave, foolishly brave, and completely foolish, which leads me to my point about fishing heroes: every self-respecting game-fishing boat that heads seaward requires the services of one or more persons with one, or all, of the above qualifications — brave, foolishly brave or completely foolish.

That poor individual is known either as the traceman or the gaff man/woman or, in cases of extreme lunacy, both; these are individuals who can perform both these skilful and extremely dangerous tasks.

These people, with scant regard for life or limb, are the last bastion of an angler against his fish after the battle that could rage for hours. These sea creatures can be so huge that they defy the imagination of even Steven Spielberg.

It is these people's job to see to it that huge marlin, sharks and tuna are brought to the side of the boat to be released, usually after an identifying tag has been stuck in them, or gaffed and killed and taken to the weigh station to be admired or booed (the latter becoming more fashionable these days) by all.

It's their job to grab hold of the wire or thick nylon trace (this can be up to nine metres in length) that is attached to the lure or bait that the fish has eaten. The other end is attached to the angler's line. In regulation game fishing, where strict rules apply, a trace is allowed to prevent the fish from escaping by biting through it or rolling in it and breaking it on its rough skin or beak. It also gives the traceman something to hang onto to bring the fish, which is more often than not going berserk by now, close enough to the boat to get a gaff into it.

More often than not these brave, foolishly brave or just plain foolish individuals have nicknames — such as Mako Bob, Gaffer Bourke,

*
1"
* OFFICIALLY RATIFIED

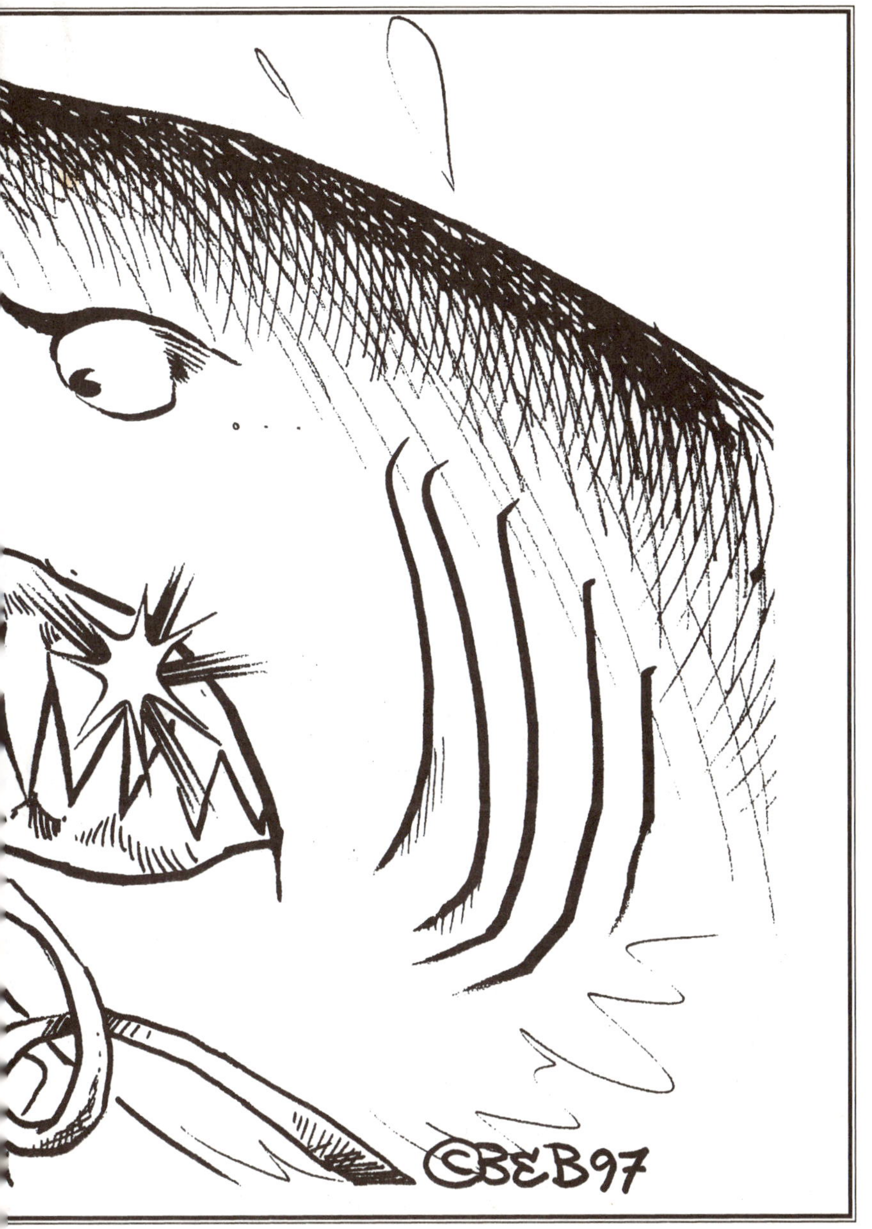
©BEB97

Great White Wally, Johnny Nine Fingers, Limbs Mackenzie and Fearless Syd — and each individual has many a tale to tell of death or near-death experiences at the fins of a mighty sea creature that they have been terrifyingly close to.

You see, the easiest part of catching a giant fish is the actual angling itself. The individual who sits in the chair and cranks the reel handle and pays the bills usually gets all the glory, but it's the skipper and crew who really do all the hard work, particularly on charter vessels where, in most cases, the paying customers wouldn't know the difference between a kingfish and a ling fish.

By far the most dangerous action is at the end of the battle: at the side of the boat, when the fish has to be traced and brought close enough to be either tagged and released or gaffed.

Tagging them is hard and dangerous enough, but sticking giant flying-gaff hooks, which are attached to ropes secured around the stem of the game chair, into huge sharks (especially white pointers, tigers and makos) or marlin, is another thing again.

Noted Australian game-fishing author and the world's foremost authority on game fishing, Peter Goadby, is a member of one of the most exclusive clubs on earth, 'The Underwater Traceman's Club', which you can only join by being dragged over the side of the boat by a huge fish as you hang onto the trace.

Goadby, who was dragged into the briny by a 500 kilogram black marlin, is one of a very select few who have survived to tell the tale. It is suspected that there are many other eligible members throughout the world, but they are too embarrassed to come forward and claim membership.

But without a doubt, the most horrifying fishing experience is wiring or gaffing a big shark. Tigers and whites roll up in the trace and flying-head gaff ropes, and makos jump clear of the water in an effort to break free.

Back in the old days, when I used to kill sharks, I was almost killed myself when a 400 kilogram mako shark I gaffed jumped the entire length (five metres) of the gaff rope and almost came into the boat.

I recall it snapping and snarling about an inch from my face and, let me tell you, its breath was so vile it could have put out a bushfire on the *Oriana*. The shark landed on one of the other crewmen's hand on the skirting board, breaking it.

The late Jack Farrell used to tell me stories of huge white pointers and tiger sharks that would roll up in the traces and gaff ropes 'like a giant, aquatic yoyo, Paul,' he would say as I listened, spellbound. 'Bob (Dyer) would play a huge tiger or white pointer to the side of the boat and it was our job to trace, gaff and secure it to the boat so we could take it back to the weigh station for the spectators to look at.'

And while the tales of these heroic deeds of the sea are many, sadly, some of the incidents are fatal. Overseas, a traceman took a couple of wraps on the wire as a small marlin of around 150 kilograms was played to the boat. Unfortunately for him, he got caught up in the trace as the marlin turned and headed for the depths. Neither of them was ever seen again.

But the greatest of them all would have to be the legendary Sydney gaffman, Ray 'The Gaffer' Bourke, who I crewed with on Keith Whitehead's 35-foot Bertram *Splashdown* for donkeys' years, and who performed some of the most extraordinary and fearless gaffing feats in the history of offshore angling.

The Gaffer was (and still is) a big lump of a bloke who managed the Forbes Club, an illegal gambling casino in Kings Cross in the '60s and '70s. The Gaffer saw more action in a night than most folks would see in a dozen lifetimes, and when it came to a bit of bravado, The Gaffer was ready for anything . . . and that most certainly included ornery critters like marlin and sharks.

One of his favourite tricks was to gaff small marlin of 50–60 kilograms in mid-air as they jumped on the trace at the back of the boat. The Gaffer would just reach out with a long-handed fixed-head gaff, anticipate where the fish was going to jump out of the water as the traceman (usually me) hung on for grim death, and then just pluck 'em out of mid-air and into the boat.

To The Gaffer, that was the end of his job, so he'd grab a cold can of Resch's and piss off up onto the flying bridge with the skipper and leave our lady deckie, Aileen Malone, and myself with a very annoyed marlin in the cockpit while he and the skipper abused us for getting blood all over the boat. The blood was usually Aileen's or mine.

Another one of The Gaffer's tricks was to hang around the berley pot, which was secured to the stern of the boat, while we were berleying and drifting for sharks, gaff at the ready. If a small mako of say 50–60 kilograms came sniffin' around the pot, The Gaffer wouldn't tell a soul; he'd just reach out with the fixed-head gaff, drag the mako on board before it knew what had happened, and throw it at anyone who just happened to be nearby.

If you've ever seen a little mako, gaffed green and in a rotten mood, going ballistic and jumping and snapping its razor-sharp fangs into anything (including stainless steel, wood, iron, plastic and humans), then you would know that being in a cockpit with one was not a good place to be.

This day The Gaffer chucked one weighing about 40 kilograms onto a poor innocent car dealer, Ray 'Snorks' Brown, who just happened to be along for the ride. The only sharks Snorks had ever seen before in his life were the blokes he worked with. The Gaffer lobbed the mako at Snorks's feet. It bit him on the leg and then chased him around the cockpit for half an hour, snapping at him and smashing everything in sight with its tail.

The Gaffer thought it was great fun until Snorks, who was no spring chicken, clutched his heart — the skipper, Keith Whitehead, ordered the shark thrown out of the boat before we had a corpse on our hands.

But this is the best story of them all. The Gaffer gaffed a marlin beneath the water, and there was no way breathing that he could lift it into the boat. The Gaffer's legendary status had come about mainly because of his strength and bulk — he could lift any fish straight into the boat, whereas other gaff men of similar status would have to seek help. Not The Gaffer. Crash, in with the gaff into a marlin and then straight into the cockpit with it in one move. The Gaffer was famous for it.

Mind you, these feats were performed off Sydney and Port Stephens, 300 kilometres north of Sydney, and the black and striped marlin we caught back in those days rarely went more than 75 kilograms, which was well within The Gaffer's lifting capacity.

This day Aileen had played a very busy little black marlin of around 60 kilograms to the back of the boat and moved back in the cockpit to allow The Gaffer to do his thing.

Whack! In went the gaff with deadly accuracy and The Gaffer pulled on the handle to drag the fish aboard. But nothing happened. The fish wouldn't budge. No matter how hard he tried, The Gaffer couldn't move the fish an inch.

The Gaffer got the shits well and truly. His unblemished record was at stake! But no matter how hard he pulled, huffing and puffing, he couldn't budge that little marlin. It was tragic to see him give up. The Gaffer's reputation was in tatters. He was a broken man. He sat in the cockpit, head in his hand, weary and beaten by this mysterious fish. It was such an emotional moment that our skipper, Keith Whitehead, actually got off his backside, and came down from the flying bridge to console him while Aileen and I held onto the gaff, and the fish that was still on the end of it, concealed beneath the hull of the boat.

'I'm not sure, Gaffer,' Whitehead said, looking over the side at the fish, 'but I think your reputation as the world's best gaffer is still intact. In fact, I think you've improved on it.'

The Gaffer looked up. 'Whadda ya mean?' he said.

'No wonder you couldn't lift the fish. You gaffed it so hard that the gaff went straight through it and into the hull of the boat. You've been trying to lift a 17-ton Bertram into its own cockpit!'

The Gaffer's reputation was indeed intact, and still is. There has never been and never will be another Gaffer Bourke. Some things aren't meant to be changed.

So here's to the legendary Gaffer Bourke and the other brave men (and the occasional woman) of his kind with limbs missing, nervous twitches, eye patches, scars and an obvious desire to be killed at sea.

The unsung heroes of fishing.

Heli-fishing to Adventure

Of all of the adventurers in the world there's none more interesting than my lifelong friend Captain Dennis 'Brazakka' Wallace. Marlin captain, helicopter pilot, skydiver, deer rancher, scuba diver and full-time maniac. I went along on a heli-fishing adventure I shall never forget.

There are four things that I'm not fussed about — snakes, spiders, guns and killing animals — and here I was in the middle of the whole lot of 'em. I could see my life flashing before me.

'There they are,' big Billy McLeod, a '90s version of Chips Rafferty, had said. He pointed as I strained my eyes from the back seat of the four-seater Robinson 44 chopper to get my first glimpse of a mobile line of black dots that was a feral pig family on the march.

It was a procession of wild *Babes*, about fifteen of 'em, trunking and tailing across an open sandy causeway that led from one heavily vegetated island to another in the vast interconnecting network of swamplands that made up this porkers' paradise. We were on the outskirts of a private cattle station inland from the sea on the eastern side of Cape York, in far northern Queensland.

As the chopper banked in for a closer look, the black dots picked up speed and for all the world resembled a line of ever-diminishing ducks on the hallway wall of a Sydney suburban semidetached.

At the head were nana and pop, then mum and dad, then the grand-kids, followed up in the rear by the great-grand-kids. Four generations of the scourge of northern Australia on the run, and big Billy was going to do his bit for conservation and blast the whole lot of them into next week.

'I'll drop you guys off on that island up ahead, the one they're heading for,' said our pilot, Captain Dennis 'Brazakka' Wallace, marlin fisherman, hunter and adventurer.

'Paul, throw your cameras around your neck and jump out with Billy when I tell you. After I've dropped you guys off, I'm going to circle back and herd 'em toward you and round up the stragglers and the ones that try and get away.

'Make sure you're ready with the cameras, 'cos Billy'll start pickin' 'em off as soon as they hit the island and I'm safely way to buggery out of there.'

I didn't have a chance to protest, or even contemplate what was in the undergrowth on that island. It looked as if I was going to die, and I wasn't even going to know what sort of snake or spider it was that bit me.

And then we were there, dumped straight into knee-high undergrowth. If Elle Macpherson was 100 metres away in the nude beckoning to me and the only thing between us was knee-high undergrowth, I'd never get to see that magnificent body up close. I hate undergrowth and all the creepy-crawlies that live in it.

As soon as the chopper hit the ground, big Billy was off and running through the undergrowth, a box of shells the size of roll-on deodorants in one hand, a silver 270 Ruger bolt-action rifle in the other, and me desperately trying to fill his every footprint and at the same time stop my cameras from swinging full circle around my neck.

My heart was jumping out of my chest.

Billy propped behind a bush and loaded the bazooka. 'Just stick with me,' he mumbled, obviously under the delusion that I might wander off and take in the sights. No chance. I was sticking to him like crap to a curtain.

'And keep quiet,' he growled. 'They're heading straight towards us and I'm gunna get the big bastards first. Don't let 'em know we're here.'

Having no idea what to expect, except that any second now I was going to be witness to wholesale slaughter, I readied my camera with the wide angle and tried to control the gasping that was forcing my heart out of my mouth.

Then they were upon us, running straight at Billy, oinking and

puffing and oblivious to the fact that in a minute or two they would all be spare ribs for their relatives to gorge themselves on over the next day or two.

KABOOOM! As the first of the herd hit dry ground about twenty yards in front of him, Billy let fly with the cannon off the *Missouri* and a giant boar with gravy-stained six-inch tusks, still running, lurched toward me and sprawled almost at my feet, squealing and farting as blood sprayed high into the air from the gaping wound in its neck. It shook its trotters for a second or two, looked up at me and died.

I wanted to throw up but I didn't have the time. KABOOM! Nana hit the deck minus half her head. KABOOM, KABOOM, mum and dad were dispatched and it was time to reload and finish off the kids. Fifteen shots — fifteen dead pigs.

It was like a scene out of *Apocalypse Now* with me as Dennis Hopper clicking away among the gunsmoke, the stench of av-gas and the whirling of the descending chopper, surrounded by death, too shell-shocked to talk; instead, letting the camera tell the tale.

I was a gibbering mess as I crawled back into the chopper, leaving the carnage in my wake. 'Looks like you got the lot, Billy,' Brazakka said casually. 'We'll come back here tomorrow. Those carcasses are terrific bait, Paul. We'll get a bunch of their best friends eating 'em tomorrow.

'Bloody filthy things. They're riddled with disease and when they're not taking calves they're rooting up the environment. Can't shoot enough of the bastards for my money. All right, boys. How about we go and catch a fish.'

That suited me down to the ground.

I was halfway through the first day of a three-day heli-fishing and hunting safari, courtesy of Brazakka. 'Better get your arse up here and take some pictures and write a few stories about my new venture,' he had told me over the phone from his deer ranch on the Atherton Tableland, just out of Cairns.

Better known as one of the top black marlin skippers in the world, anything Brazakka does is news, and I've been taking pictures and writing stories about him and his adventures for donkeys' years.

I knew that the heli-fishing and hunting safaris would be like anything else Brazakka put his hand to — action-packed adventure and bundles of fun.

'I'm running three-day safaris out of Cairns into Cape York for two clients at a time to fish and hunt,' he told me. 'It's about as much action as anyone can cope with in three days and we cover more territory than you'd ever see out of a 4WD in two weeks. You'll get some great shots.'

He wasn't wrong. We had left Cairns that morning and flown along the coast to Cooktown, our first stop for fuel. Big Billy McLeod, ace angler, crack shot and an authority on Cape York and its fishing holes, was along for the ride, pointing out places of interest he had either fished or hunted over the years.

We'd stopped briefly on the golden sands of Princess Charlotte Bay for a feed of prawns Billy had brought with him, and then we flew on up the coast, noting the best spots to fish — where the tidal rivers and creeks feed into the ocean and the barramundi, king salmon, mangrove jacks and tarpon lie in wait as the bait fish are forced out with the tide.

'The run-out isn't until mid-afternoon,' Billy had calculated. 'Let's go and kill us a few pigs while we wait.'

And kill pigs Billy did until it was time to head back to the coast and catch the fish napping while they were waiting for afternoon tea on the turn of the tide.

'That spot should do us,' said Brazakka, pointing to a big lagoon with fast-running water and a 15-foot croc basking on the sand, obviously guarding its manor against unwelcome intruders. As we came in to land, it opened its gob, which could have passed for the entrance to Luna Park, hissed at us and slid into the drink, clearly not keen to challenge the chopper.

'It's great that we've seen that horrible bastard,' said Billy as Brazakka landed right next to the huge webbed footprints in the sand. 'He knows *we're* here and we know *he's* here,' he laughed. 'He's just as frightened of us as we are of him and now it's a standoff.'

'We're safe to fish here until he figures out some sort of a game plan to get us,' Billy continued, as he reached down to wash his hands where the footprints disappeared into the lagoon. I felt the hairs on the back of my neck stand on end.

I had visions of the croc materialising out of the water in front of him, Crocodile Dundee/Linda Kozlowski style, and Brazakka running in and stabbing it in the head with a bowie knife. This pair would probably get off on something like that.

'He's probably over there in the mangroves, sulking,' Billy pointed, now standing ankle-deep in the same spot. 'You can bet your life that if we came back here every day at the same time, after three or four days that old croc would have it all figured out.

'He'd be waiting just under the surface at the water's edge or somewhere behind one of us, ready to charge and take us with him into the lagoon. They're cunning bastards, but it takes 'em a while to put it together. We'll be long gone by then.'

Billy cast his Rapala 'Husky Jerk' lure toward a submerged tree that acted as perfect cover for the ambushing barras, cranked the Shimano 400 Baitcaster into gear, wound the handle a couple of turns and hooked up to a four kilogram barra — just like that.

'Yeah, Brazak, they're on,' he mumbled nonchalantly to his mate, who by now had a lure in the water and was also hooked up. 'They should be bitin' their heads off for about another half hour or so and then they'll go off the bite at the bottom of the tide.'

And guess what? They did.

I suppose we caught about twenty in that session. It was almost a fish a throw. They were so thick that I even put down the camera and caught one myself, my first.

And then, as Billy and Brazakka very well knew would happen, there were none. Time to move on.

That night we stayed at an outstation on a remote cattle ranch, drank beer with the locals, dined on steak, eggs and chips, and slept like dead people.

After a huge breakfast the following morning, washed down with real tea made in a big pot with good old-fashioned tea-leaves floating around in it, it was time for some jungle creek fishing for barramundi, jungle perch, sooty grunter and mangrove jacks.

This is adventure fishing at its best and most difficult: hiking through thick undergrowth, looking for lagoons in a river that has long been landlocked, with the fish trapped until the wet season arrives early in the year and the rains fill the river to overflowing and run it and its inhabitants into the sea.

The hardest part is finding enough room to cast your lure at a snag, which is where the barra and jacks like to ambush. Getting to these aquariums in a 4WD is all but impossible, but in a helicopter it's possible to fish lagoons that no man has ever fished before. We caught a stack of jacks and barra that day in about twenty different spots.

That night we stayed at a country pub, ate some of the fish we had caught that day for dinner, washed them down with a couple of cold bottles of sauvignon blanc and slept in airconditioned comfort in bunkhouse-style accommodation. Country livin' at its best.

Day three we fished and hunted our way home, this time shooting pigs on the flat, almost grassless, savannas. This made taking pictures a lot easier, even if I did have one eye through the lens and the other on the lookout for taipans.

We explored running rivers and creeks and drank crystal-clear water from rocky mountain streams and cast lures into the lagoons.

Lunch on the last day was yet another of the many highlights of the trip. We called into a remote fishing camp on the Annie River, and straight out of the pot we ate delicious warm mud crabs with fresh bread and butter and washed them down with some icy-cold beers.

The muddies had been caught and cooked especially for us that morning. It's all part of the deal. The old Brazakka doesn't miss a trick when it comes to giving his clients the trip of a lifetime.

If there is a problem with the trip, it's that so much happens in the three days that it's hard to remember what happened a few hours earlier. Usually hunting and fishing just don't go hand in hand, even though most hunters are anglers and vice versa. Combine the two with the convenience of a chopper and it's the once-in-a-lifetime blow-out, even for an old city slicker like me.

The Hunt Comes Up Trump

Dogs and fishing go together like cats and milk. They have certainly been a part of my fishing life and I've fished on many a boat where a dog has been a member of the crew. My search for the ultimate Aussie fishing dog came up Trumps.

To my mind, dogs are about the most humorous critters in the world and they are as much a part of fishing as your rod and reel. You know the old saying: 'A dog is man's best friend because he wags his tail and not his tongue.'

Not that they do much to help us catch fish, but there's always a dog to be found somewhere in a typical Aussie fishing scene.

The classic cartoon of the scruffy kid on his way through the bush to his favourite spot with a fishing pole over his shoulder, a jar of tadpoles and the inevitable dog at his heels says it all.

The first European dog to lift his leg on Australian soil was a Newfoundland mutt named Hector, who came here with the First Fleet and was owned by John Marshall, master of the 450-ton convict transport *Scarborough.*

I wonder if it was just coincidence that Marshall chose a Newfoundland — or was it because they were the original fishing dogs that went to sea on fishing boats and were trained to swim out to the nets heavy with salmon and help the fishermen drag them in?

Did the wise old ship's master anticipate there would be fish aplenty in the new land and that Hector could help catch them?

Sir Joseph Banks certainly didn't have fishing on his mind when he chose his canine companion for the voyage. At Foreshore Park in Botany Bay, a monument celebrating the fleet's arrival shows Banks examining flora and fauna, and at his feet there is a dog — probably a whippet, but most certainly not a fishing dog.

But while dogs can be great fishing companions, they can also be bloody pests. I'd like a dollar for every time one has piddled on my fishing bag or run off with the lunch Mum so painstakingly put together.

Years ago there was a dog that used to haunt the wharf at Kurnell on the southern side of Botany Bay. He would pinch the bait and eat it and didn't care if there was a hook in it or not. Anglers got sick of taking hooks out of the poor old fella but he never learned from the experience. They would take half-a-dozen hooks out of him one night and he'd be back there the next day for more.

The luckiest ocean-going pooch alive is a four-year-old German shepherd bitch named Lizzy, who was found swimming six kilometres off Queensland's Sunshine Coast by two fishermen last November. She was claimed by her relieved owners the following day. They said Lizzy had fallen unnoticed off their yacht and they had given up any hope of seeing her again. The very exhausted Lizzy had been in the shark-infested waters for about six hours before she was rescued.

And then there was Rex the Wonder Dog, who lived at the Gap Tavern on top of the cliffs at the famous suicide spot at Sydney's Watsons Bay. Many a time Rex saved the lives of potential suiciders by grabbing their clothing and dragging them back from the cliffs as they stood and contemplated the 120-metre jump.

Buster the fishing dog was the toast of the coast when he performed the most extraordinary rescue while fishing with his master, Gary Nicholson, off the high rocks at Malabar Point on the northern shores of Botany Bay.

Buster and Gary were fishing away when a nearby rockhopper made such a forceful cast that his rod flew from his hands and landed in the drink. The ever-alert Buster leapt into the water, grabbed the rod between his teeth and braved a dreadful buffeting on the rocks to drop the rod and reel back at the amazed angler's feet.

So with all of these 'dog fishing facts and stories' in mind, I set out on a quest to find Sydney's fishiest dog. With my cameras whirring, I searched the beaches and wharves, and though I found plenty of dogs hanging about, none of them had the qualifications to be immortalised in a fishing story book.

I let my friends know what I was looking for. A dog that was up to its eyeballs in anything that involved fish.

A pretty tall ask? It sure was, but if I was going to go to the trouble to take the pictures and write the story, then the canine had to have something special.

A fishy dog that went out on trawlers, or helped serve behind the counter at the fishmarkets, perhaps wrestled crocodiles, maybe stood guard at the Oceanarium, or rode a surf ski while his master trolled a handline off the back, would have been ideal. But no such luck.

And then, just when I was about to give up, I found Trump.

Trump is a seven-year-old Dalmatian-blue heeler, who lives with the Franks family — Norelle, husband Bill, and daughter Camilla — at Sydney's Watsons Bay. He's a docile old slug, probably due to his being grossly obese.

Norelle reckons that if Trump went to Jenny Craig, they would only give him a quote. And there's a very good reason for Trump's porky condition, but more about that in a minute.

Trump's a real party dog and at functions at home, he waddles from guest to guest for a pat and doesn't mind getting dressed up as long as it gets him plenty of attention.

And without a doubt, Trump's fishing outfit is his favourite. He'll sit for hours in his gamefishing cap, sunnies, vest, rod and reel just to cop all the attention from family and friends. And, naturally, the odd handout.

And why wouldn't Trump love fish and fishing? After all, his staple diet is the best seafood in Australia. Trump lives a stone's throw from Doyle's famous Watsons Bay seafood restaurant and at any lunchtime he can be found on the promenade botting the delicious offerings from Doyle's patrons.

Little wonder he's so fat he can hardly walk. Chips, fish, crabs and lobster — Trump gets to sample the lot as generous diners fall for the big brown eyes and the slobbering 'I'll go away if you give me a bit' look. And believe me, it's in the diner's best interest to give Trump something to eat and see him on his way because the sight of him slobbering giant globules all down his chin is enough to put anyone off their lunch, even a famous Doyle's lunch. No, it's not a pretty sight.

One customer even put a note around his neck which read: 'Mum, please don't feed me tonight because I might be sick. I've been eating fish and chips all day and I couldn't possibly be hungry.' Trump wasn't.

Norelle says that Trump never eats at home anyway. He's too busy socialising and having lunch. When he gets home he's so exhausted he takes his ballooning carcass to bed — and probably dreams about botting seafood at Doyle's the next day.

I wouldn't mind coming back as Trump in the next life. No work, no dieting, no money worries, lots of love and the best seafood in the country every day.

The guy who said it's a dog's life obviously hadn't met Trump.

The Loaded Croc

This story is Sydney eastern suburbs folklore, and while the variations of it are many, this is the fair dinkum version. Though conspicuous by their absence in recent years, the main characters are real and the story never came to light until long after the incident — one day they had a monumental altercation at the Royal Oak Hotel and one blurted out just how stupid his mate was and gave this story as an example.

We christened him 'Haemorrhoids' because he hung out in dark places. We broke it down to 'Piles' for short. One of those dark places he hung out in was the Royal Oak Hotel in Double Bay in Sydney's eastern suburbs, where he was a member of the legendary Royal Oak Fishing Club.

He was a short, bald, unshaven, revoltingly fat heap with a Charles Bronson drooping moustache who wore Stubbies and a footy jumper every day, guzzled vast quantities of beer and wore out two pairs of thongs a month.

Eastern suburbs folklore had it that one day when he was lying on Bondi beach, the Greenpeace truck came to a grinding halt and six guys rushed out and tried to force him back into the water.

The only person who could cop him was a bloke we'd nicknamed 'Morphine' on account of the fact that he was a slow-working dope. Morph was as long and lean as Piles was short and rotund, wore a Sydney Swans beanie, checked long-sleeved flannelette shirts, bell-bottomed trousers and ugh boots all year round.

They looked like Abbott and Costello, but it was impossible to imagine them doing a classic routine such as 'Who's On First'; that was way out of their depth.

Piles and Morph were inseparable, quaffing down schooners night after night over the pool table at the Oak. And when they weren't playing pool or figuring out how to get away with more sickies from their jobs on the local council, they filled out their weekly Lotto coupon, methodically double- and triple-checking to make sure that they got their lucky numbers — which, incidentally, were the same every week — exactly right.

They figured they had the winning combination by using the numbers that meant the most to them. Their birth dates; 16 and 24: their ages; 37 and 39: their IQs; 28 and 28: their past lovers; 0 and 0: and their friends; 1 and 1, being each other.

So that was the combination: 16, 24, 37, 39, 28, 0 and 1 as the supplementary. Week in and week out they took the same numbers and every Monday night the Oak would come to a standstill as the beautiful Alex Wileman called the numbers with the three Lotteries officials looking on.

But they never won a crumpet. In fact, the best they ever got was two numbers. But their faith in their system was unfailing.

This particular Monday, Morph had taken a sickie off work, got on the piss all day and took it upon himself to fill in the Lotto numbers before having a dozen or so more schooners at the Oak while waiting for his mate to come in after work.

When Morph produced their ticket at Lotto time, Piles nearly had a stroke.

'You fuckin' idiot,' he exploded. 'You've written out the wrong numbers. I couldn't trust you to take a piss by yourself. You can bet your fuckin' life that they'll go off tonight and we won't be on 'em.'

With that he grabbed a snooker cue in one hand and Morph by the throat with the other and was just about to fracture his dopey mate's skull with it when Alex Wileman called out the first number — 17.

'Hey, that's one of your bodgie numbers,' Piles noted, lowering the cue and taking interest. 'Number 4,' the sensational Alex Wileman gushed as Piles noted that that number was also on the ticket.

And so was the next one, and the next one after that and the one after that. They had the first five numbers in and the Oak was hushed

PARDON

BOOM!

in anticipation and then went berserk as Alex called the sixth number and it matched the ticket.

The Dickbrain Brothers had won Lotto by default, but Morph wasn't letting on that it was a fluke.

'It's me new scientific system of gettin' the numbers,' he told anyone stupid enough to listen. I'd had 17 schooners when I bought the ticket; me nephew's four next birthday . . .' and so on . . . crap on, jerk off, bullshit, wank . . . Of course no one with an eighth of a brain took any notice.

There turned out to be three other winners, and by the time the four split the $1.5 million Lotto first prize, Piles and Morph had enough to buy the best Toyota 4WD, camping gear and 'trailerable' boat that money could buy and they decided to go on an extended fishing vacation into northern Australia, much to our eternal gratitude.

'That'll teach youse pricks to take the piss out of us,' Piles announced down at the Oak on the eve of their departure. 'Me and me genius mate 'ere, Morph, is gunna shoot through to the Northern Territory and get stuck into the barramundis and none of youse billygoats is welcome.'

And thank Christ for that. Peace from the boneheads at last. Even if it was only temporary.

It took Piles and Morphine six days to reach Darwin, where they loaded up with cases of beer and supplies and headed for the Mary River. They found a great big barra-filled tidal lagoon and set up camp.

What a treat. No bastard for miles, stacks of ice in the freezer for the beer, no sheilas to drive 'em mad and a hole full of fish. Heaven on earth. Well, not quite.

There was just one minor problem — the old croc who'd made the huge billabong his home for the past 30 years. The cranky old bastard was far from impressed with his new neighbours and expressed his disapproval by nicking every decent-sized fish they hooked.

'There's that fuckin' mobile suitcase at it again,' Morphine would blubber to his mate as the croc sat waiting for a jumping barra to land in its giant, foul-smelling gobhole.

'I wish he'd fuck off and leave us alone,' moaned Piles as he lost yet another barra, a $15 lure and lots of line to the croc.

But they were reluctant to move on, because the fishing — minus the croc — was superb. Besides, there would most likely be a resident croc wherever they wound up. One or the other had to go and sooner or later something had to give. It did.

'Have you noticed how he shoots through every night about six?' noted Piles, his skills of observation working overtime. 'I reckon he goes back to the missus in the lair, chunders up some of the fish he's pinched from us and feeds 'em to 'er, gives her a good root and then they pack it in for the night.'

'The dirty bastard — I'd like to blow his scaly old cock off while he's on the job!'

They laughed hilariously at the thought of two crocodiles hard at it, and wondered if they tongue-kissed each other while they were doing it, what with their putrid breath and all.

Neither of them was renowned for his powers of deduction, so while the thought of a prehistoric animal living to a timetable would be absurd to most of us, it certainly wasn't to Piles and his dopey mate. Instead, it gave one of them an idea.

'Speakin' of blowin' the bastard's eight-day-clock off, you've given me a real good idea,' Piles chuckled to his mate. 'Let's go into town tomorrow and I'll get somethin' that might just sort our problem right out. He'll be a cockless croc come dusk.'

In town the following morning, they loaded up with supplies, then ducked into the hardware store. They bought a case of dynamite and all the other ingredients which they needed to blow up fish-stealing, prehistoric reptiles.

'Do you really think it'll work?' Morph asked his mate, plainly in awe of the brilliant scheme.

'Course it will,' said Piles. 'We wait until the bastard comes up for his last fish of the arvo and we'll chuck him a couple of nicely iced-off barra from out of the Esky under the 4WD.

'Only this time they'll have enough dynamite attached to blow up fuckin' Ayers Rock.

'Once the greedy prick of a thing has swallowed the lot, we'll let him swim off with the fuse wire trailing out of his gob and when he stops we'll wait for a while till we reckon he's on the job and then we'll light it, and give his missus the biggest bang she's ever had.'

They laughed outrageously at their scheme and went about fishing from the bank well down the river from their campsite and preparing themselves for the afternoon's events. And, as if on cue, the croc did his bit by turning up and pinching their fish all day long.

'Go on, make the most of it, ya fuckin' turd of a thing,' Morph abused the old croc from the bank. 'Ya might as well, seein' as today's ya last day on this planet. In a coupla hours your head's gunna be in Darwin and your cock's gunna be in Alice Springs.'

Mid-afternoon they returned to camp, grabbed a couple of nice cold barramundi from the Esky under the 4WD and taped four sticks of dynamite to them.

Just on six they hooked a beaut fish that brought the croc within feeding range, and as it gulped the leaping barra down, Piles threw the dynamited fish at him and he gulped those down too.

'The silly prick's fallen for it,' laughed Morphine. 'You're a bloody genius, Piles. Now let's wait for a while and we'll teach the bastard to pinch our fish.'

So they sat on the bank and watched as the waterproofed fuse wire steadily disappeared from the giant coil and into the water as the Croc headed off upstream.

They'd brought plenty of beer and it was only a five-minute trip by boat back to camp. They yarned the time away as the croc kept on the move.

'It'll be interestin' just to see where the explosion goes off,' said Piles. 'Christ, he must have 1000 metres of fuse wire out by now. One thing's for certain — the big bang won't be close to us.'

Then the croc stopped. They waited for a couple of minutes, then lit the fuse and watched the smoke snake down the bank and into the water.

'I hope he's right in the middle of a Wellington boot and on the

vinegar stroke when it goes off,' roared Piles. 'That'll give 'is missus an orgasm the likes of which Crocville has never seen before!'

Then it happened. The bank shook as a huge explosion rocked the earth all around and a mushroom-shaped ball of smoke belched high into the sky from downriver — in the direction of the camp.

They took off in the boat at breakneck speed amid falling debris, mostly flesh and blood.

'Jesus, that was a big bit,' Piles gulped at a huge splash near them. 'And it didn't look like blown-up croc, riverbed or stump to me. It looked more like a gearbox. A Toyota gearbox.'

Morphine ducked just in time to miss being decapitated by a flying steering wheel. And as they raced toward camp they realised that their worst nightmare had come to pass.

'You fuckin' idiot!' screamed Morph at Piles.

'You gave that croc the taste for cold barramundi and the bastard's crawled up to the Esky for more and you've blown the bloody 4WD into the Kimberley. Now how are we gunna get home?'

As it turned out, that was the least of their worries. That evening they were arrested for violations of the *Protection of Crocodiles Act* and their return to Double Bay was interrupted by a short stay in the Darwin nick.

Both Morphine and Haemorrhoids are barred from the Northern Territory for life.

Lureitis . . . Fishing's Deadliest Disease

There are many known fishing addictions and diseases . . . with few known cures. Lying, boasting and cheating are among the most common. But the most horrific of them all is the piscatorial disease of the '80s and '90s . . . the cruelly incurable, totally addictive, outrageously expensive and often life-threatening addiction known throughout the fishing community as . . . *Lureitis.* Does someone close to you have this ghastly affliction? How would you know if they did? Read on and find out about the piscatorial plague that is a distinct threat to any angler who goes near a fishing tackle shop.

Browsing through the huge range of lures on sale in a tackle shop recently, I couldn't help but wonder just where it is all going to end. I mean, just how many lures can they make? Just how many different shapes and sizes can the market absorb? After all, there are only so many lure fishermen out there.

Or are there?

The market seems insatiable and I believe that it's due to the fact that most of the lures sold never see the light of day, let alone get wet or, heaven forbid, get bitten by a fish.

Crikey, we couldn't have that now, could we? Use one of those fantastic creations to actually try and catch a fish? No way.

I believe that there is a secret Lure Society out there. That's right. A clandestine gaggle of Australia's newest menace to society — lure gatherers. Folk who are constantly preoccupied with a pastime as addictive as narcotics and around about the same price for a fix.

Is your husband, mate, brother or son one of them? Do you suspect that the old man has got another woman or a shipment of dirty magazines? Does he sneak out at odd hours and lock himself in the garage or study and make long, orgasmic, moaning noises? Does he talk to his mates in a dialect unknown to you that constantly refers to 'bibbed minnows', 'deep divers', 'fizzers', 'poppers' and 'mid-water runners'?

He does? Well, you poor wretch, you've got my sympathy. Your loved one's got *Lureitis,* and old Dr Kidd's here to tell you that it's incurable. If this highly addictive disease could get a guernsey in the *Macquarie*, I reckon it would read something like this:

> **lureitis** (lure-i'tis) *n*, incurable disease involving overwhelming infatuation with fishing lures, usually contracted by fisherfolk and fishing tackle shop staff; no known cure. Symptoms: red bulging eyes from staring at walls and walls of lures in fishing tackle shops and department stores, absence during the night for long periods at a time (this time is usually spent fondling lures in garage or den). Treatment: take victim to as many fishing tackle shops as possible and let him gaze at the lures for long periods. When he starts frothing at the mouth, blubbering and pointing, buy him the lure he is pointing at and lock him in a well-lit room with it until moaning subsides. Outside of that it is hopeless; death usually occurs by drowning as the addict dives out of the boat to retrieve a beloved lure that is caught on a snag; addicts are also regularly taken by crocodiles when performing impossible recovery techniques.

Yup, it's as bad as that. I've known blokes to let their families go without food and clothing, spending the money instead on artificial fish enticements. Normal blokes are doing time in the slammer for breaking into tackle shops in the dead of night to steal lures. Blokes who normally wouldn't get so much as a parking fine are doing time as habitual lure thieves.

It won't be long now before someone sets up Lures Anonymous to try and cure these poor wretches of this horrid addiction. There they

TREAT THIS LURE LIKE A BABY OR I'LL KILL YOU...
GIMME GIMME GIMME

TOM'S
POP
POP

will be, Halco lure catalogues in hand, telling their fellow lure junkies how they have to face the world one day at a time. And how they have to resist the urge to go to fishing tackle shops on the slightest impulse. And that listening to others may help. Yup, it's a strange old world out there.

My introduction to *Lureitis* was back in the late '60s, when I used to fish the rocks (a form of fishing called 'spinning') for game fish such as yellowfin, striped and mackerel tuna, kingfish and salmon, using highly polished chrome lures that when retrieved rapidly, resembled a scurrying bait fish.

I formed a fishing relationship with a certain Ronnie Rimmer, rock fisherman and legendary lure-maker. Ronnie's main claim to fame was that he was the creator of the best lure I have ever used in my life for fishing the rocks.

Called the Rimmer Special, it was made of cast lead in a home-made mould, about three inches long, sliced at both ends and highly chromed. It looked for all the world like a whitebait, shimmering just beneath the surface. And they were deadly on pelagics.

Although Ronnie used to sell his lures privately, I think for about a buck each in those days, he always parted with them with a certain amount of reluctance, sort of like a breeder selling off a litter of pups.

'Now you make sure you look after them,' Ronnie would tell the purchaser as he fondled the lures before handing them over to their new owner. 'Lot of work went into them. Treat 'em right and you'll get lots of fish.'

And true to his faith in his own product, Ronnie pounded the oceans daily from the rocks with his beloved Rimmer Specials, telling anyone who would listen that the shape of them was a special aerodynamic design that sent the fish bonkers. Those lures were like Ronnie's kids, and he loved them with a passion.

Yup. Ronnie had the worst case of *Lureitis* I'd ever seen, but in those days I had no idea what it was. He used to talk about his lures the way Bubba talked about shrimp in *Forrest Gump*. The poor bastard had it real bad.

But then came the day when a lure broke poor Ronnie's heart — I

have never seen or heard of him from that day to this. To him it must have seemed like a death in the family.

This day we were spinning side by side at Ben Buckler, on Bondi Beach's northern end, casting our lures up to 120 yards out to sea and then retrieving them rapidly on our highly geared reels so as to make the lures resemble scurrying bait fish and entice the pelagics to bite them. Ronnie's lure had just hit the water and as he clunked his old Mitchell 499 into gear and took a turn of the handle, he found himself fast to a big fish.

It took off like a burning dog, testing the drag on Ronnie's reel to the limit, and just as it seemed that it would empty his spool, he turned the big fish and the fight was on.

'Big yellowfin, I reckon,' he groaned as he lay back into his giant fishing rod, much to the awe of the Sunday crowd that had started to gather in the car park about a hundred feet above us.

'Certainly bigger than anything I've ever had on before. Jeez, those little darlin' lures of mine just never let me down. Shame they can't cook and iron. I swear blind I'd marry one of 'em.'

For about an hour or so the battle raged to and fro to the urging of the crowd, which had now swelled to a couple of hundred. At water level we couldn't see the fish but the folks up in the car park could see how big it was as it fought hard on the surface.

'It's a bloody whopper, mate,' they yelled to Ronnie who was by now loving every second of this. 'It's a bloody whale.'

And then it was at our feet. A huge yellowfin tuna of around 40 kilograms was in the wash as I readied the five-metre rock gaff to end the fight.

'Just a couple more inches, Ronnie, and it's ours,' I yelled over the cheering of the crowd. 'Just walk back slowly and bring it closer to me and I'll gaff it.'

Ronnie gingerly stepped backwards, bringing the exhausted fish inch by inch closer to the gaff, as I reached out to full arm's length. Just as I prepared the long rock gaff for the coup de grâce, something gave way and Ronnie fell over backwards — I had to watch helplessly, to the groaning of the crowd, as the huge fish swam away.

'What the bloody hell?' Ronnie screamed, 'Don't tell me that after all that, the bloody line broke!'

But I hadn't heard the familiar 'twang' of nylon busting. No, it wasn't the line. A horribly disappointed Ronnie wound in his line to find, to his astonishment, that his beloved lure had broken in half.

I thought he was going to have a breakdown there and then. To him it was like finding out that his beloved wife had another bloke. Ronnie Rimmer was a shot duck.

Heartbroken and deeply wounded, Ronnie didn't utter another word. He just picked up his gear and walked off into the afternoon, never to be seen again by me.

That's about the saddest thing that could ever happen to a lure junkie.

But if there ever was a cure for *Lureitis* . . . that would have to be it.

The Fish Hit Parade — Tuna Up in the Key of Sea

What could be more logical than the music of wonderful sea noises to entice the fish? But what do you do when they get sick of the same old sounds? We should give them a choice, that's what. And if this piscatorial lunacy doesn't get you making up a few tunes yourself, then your funny bone should go into the berley pot.

Many years ago we invented the Fish Hit Parade. That's right. A piscatorial parade of pops for pilchards, piranhas, prawns, pike and perch. Crazy? Maybe. But it's also lots of fun to while away the hours when the fish aren't biting. And let's face it . . . that's usually most of the time.

It all started when I read a few years back that someone had invented this gadget that attracted tuna to the professional boats. It worked like this. They figured that if they could invent some sounds that turned the tuna on then they would follow the sound waves to the source, in this case a giant tuna trawler, and they could be caught. Instead of going to wherever the tuna were, they would bring the tuna to them.

And they did this by lowering a transmitter into the water and sending out sounds that were music to the tunas' ears, such as the sounds of millions of anchovies or pilchards boiling in the water. Or the noises of thousands of sea birds screeching and flapping their wings as they plummeted into the water to feed on the bait fish. Or the sounds of distressed fish sending out vibrations through the currents. Ingenious.

Incredible as it may seem, it worked, and the tuna would flock to the transmitter like Brown's cows. The skipper would turn the sound up

and whip them into a frenzy, then they would pole them into the boat. As simple as that.

It worked for a long time and then the tuna didn't come any more. No one could figure it out. Had they caught them all? Had they gone to warmer or colder currents?

One balmy Sunday afternoon many years later, during the New South Wales Interclub Game Fishing Tournament, we were sucking on some cold beers and trolling the current lines off Port Stephens for marlin on Keith Whitehead's *Splashdown* when someone commented on the shortage of fish and wondered where they had gone.

It reminded me of the disappearing tuna all those years ago and I told the fellas the story.

'Maybe they got sick of hearing the same music over and over again,' commented the skipper, Darcy Franklin. 'They probably woke to the fact that they were being conned and shot through. They should have played 'em something different.'

'Like what?' said deckie John Whitehead, '"Salmon Chanted Evening" perhaps, or maybe "Mullet of Kintire"?'

'How about "I Did it Mulloway"?' said Darcy, and the Fish Hit Parade was born.

We spent the rest of the day racking our brains for more and came up with the obvious ones like 'I'm Breaming Of A Whiting Christmas', 'When You Said You Loved Me I Thought I Was Herring Things', 'Twist and Trout', 'Whale Meat Again' and 'I Lobster and Never Flounder Again'.

Back at the pub we had the joint in hysterics, and the drunker we got the cornier and funnier the Fish Hit Parade became. 'Tunny Boy' brought the house down and 'Prawn Free' and 'Slimy To The Moon' had 'em rollin' in the aisles.

It was one of the funniest nights that the Country Club Hotel at Shoal Bay has ever seen.

And then the tournament was over and it was time to go home and the Fish Hit Parade was put on hold until the following year. By then it seemed to have lost its momentum, and just didn't seem as funny as it was when we invented it.

I published a short story about the Fish Hit Parade and listed the old favourites, most of which I have already mentioned. Expecting little or no response, I was bewildered when letters started pouring in from all over the country with their lists of songs to be included in a revised and updated version of the Fish Top Ten.

Andrew Campbell-Burns, of Melbourne, sent in no less than 52 titles and a Colonel Alan Durant and his mate, Patrolman Terry King, produced 32 fishy favourites.

With many thanks to them, lots of other readers and John and Darcy, I have now compiled this world exclusive — Fish Hit Parade's Twenty All-Time Classics (plus some other composers and groups who are worth a mention):

A White Cork Float And A Pink Crustacean.
Oyster Her Standing There.
On the Toad to Manta Ray.
Flake, Rattle and Troll.
I Love Her But I Just Can't Kipper Any More.
You Make My Life Halibut I'm Staying.
The Moray See You.
Yabby Road.
There's a Storm Across The Trevally.
Old Dogs And Children And Watermelon Tarwhine.
Love Is A Many Splendid Ling.
Eel Have To Go.
Kippery Doo Da, Kippery Ay.
Tell Him That You've Never Gurnard Leave Him.
If You Knew Sushi Like I Know Sushi.
Ling Went The Strings Of My Carp.
Sharking All Over.
Oh Me Marlin Clementine.
Duelling Banjo Sharks.
Somebody Sole My Gal.
Crabba Dabba Honeymoon.

Most popular composers: Simon and Garfish and Rodgers and Hammerhead.

Most popular group: The Trevallying Wilberries.

Most popular singers: Pike and Tina Tuna and Shirley Wrassey.

So the next time you're out fishing and the bites are as scarce as feathers on a frog, have a crack at the Fish Hit Parade and you'll keep yourselves in stitches all day.

Thirsty Bert

This is a true story and very much a part of the very rich Watsons Bay folklore. Sadly, the only folks who can verify the story, Curly Lewis and Jack Farrell, are fishing in another place these days. Apart from a few embellishments, this rendition of the legend is as close to the truth as can be recalled.

'Thirsty' Bert McRae loved a drink — hence the nickname. Thirsty was the local pest at the Watsons Bay Hotel, the watering hole at the fishing village inside Sydney's South Head.

Thirsty subsidised his unemployment benefits cheque by freeloading drinks off tourists in exchange for stories about the locals and their fishing adventures. Fact or fiction . . . who cared? And the drunker Thirsty got, the louder, more raucous and bizarre the stories became.

'Come on Thirsty, tell us another one,' the boggle-eyed tourists called as they plied him with more drink, and the yarns would flow until he was blind and decided it was time to go home while he was still capable.

'Home' was Curly Howard's 8-metre fishing boat *Gladys,* named after his fire-breathing old wife and moored in the bay about 100 metres off the beach, right in front of Doyle's famous seafood restaurant.

Every night Thirsty had the Doyle's patrons in hysterics as he made his way home in his tiny dinghy, standing at the back as full as a high school hatrack, rowing with the one central oar, instinctively gondoliering his way through the minefield of cabin cruisers and yachts that blocked his path.

This nightly spectacle was always best to watch in a raging southerly, when Thirsty also had to fend off boats swinging

NO THIRSTY ... THE TODAY SHOW WAS FIRST TIME ROUND ... THIS IS (HEM) THE FOREVER SHOW...
THRONE ROOM
SHOWE
HADES
RUM

WINGS
HALOS
HARPS
BAIT
LINES

dangerously on their moorings. Incredibly, he always made it, and when he got there he'd crash in his bunk and snore and fart until Curly arrived at around 2am. Then they'd head out to fish the inshore reefs for snapper and jewfish.

Curly and Thirsty had formed this amicable fishing partnership years earlier and it suited them both down to the ground. It gave Curly a chance to get away from the old death adder, and at the same time provided Thirsty with a home and plenty of fishing, his favourite pastime outside of getting pissed.

This night Thirsty had really done a shocking job on himself. A busload of Yanks had hit the Bay at about 10am and gathered Thirsty in tow. He'd entertained them all day and in return they'd fed him and kept the whisky and beer flowing until he could take no more.

At about 8pm he made the awkward evening pilgrimage out to *Gladys* and passed out on the cockpit floor, rotten. When Curly arrived at 2am loaded up with food, bait and a bottle of rum, Thirsty was just recovering from the day's events and was ready for the start of round two.

Curly fired up the noisy single diesel engine and off they went, Curly at the wheel and Thirsty sitting on the transom swigging on the bottle of rum with his feet hanging over the back.

The sea was as flat as a night carter's hat as *Gladys* headed east in search of a feed. The roaring of the big Gardener diesel engine didn't allow for much chat . . . but so what? Curly just steered and observed into the blackness ahead, drifting off from time to time into his fantasy world of giant snapper and jewfish big enough to swallow a man whole.

Thirsty might be the world's greatest lush, he thought, but he was great company and a terrific fisherman. Life was great.

Curly didn't notice Thirsty fall overboard. Rendered unconscious by the repeated swigs of raw rum, Thirsty had gone to sleep sitting on the back of the boat and fallen in.

By the time Thirsty realised what had happened, *Gladys* had disappeared into the night, the roaring engine eliminating any possibility of Curly hearing his cries for help.

Curly just kept steering ahead, oblivious to the disaster in his wake. Thirsty sobered up in an instant and coughed up a gallon of salt water from his lungs. He knew he was in deep shit.

'Bloody hell,' he thought. 'What do I do now?'

It was too far to swim home and the chance of a passing boat finding him in the dark was remote. He trod water and assessed the situation. A lifetime at sea had taught him many things.

He knew that at this time of the year the warm currents ran from the north at around one knot. He also knew that the teraglin were also on the bite at The Wreck — a popular reef about three kilometres south — and there was bound to be someone fishing there. He figured that if he just lay on his back and drifted with the current, he should bump into one of the fishing boats in about four or five hours.

'Sharks won't be a problem,' he chuckled to himself. 'I'll just breathe on the poor bastards as a deterrent.'

And so Thirsty Bert floated south on his back — and into Watsons Bay folklore — at about one knot an hour, along the way collecting large clumps of floating seaweed that added to his buoyancy.

He was having a little nap when, exactly three hours later, he bumped into a moored vessel occupied by Mad Ivan the Russian, who was busy filling the boat hand-over-fist with teraglin. The last thing Ivan was expecting was guests.

If he had lost all else in those years of alcohol-induced haze, Thirsty had maintained his manners. Rather than clamber aboard someone else's boat unannounced, he knocked on the hull the same way he would knock on someone's front door.

Mad Ivan shit himself and, armed with a boat-hook, proceeded to attack the seaweed-encrusted sea monster clinging to the side of his boat until it uttered: ''Scuse me mate, you wouldn't happen to be going anywhere near Watsons Bay, would you?'

Hauled aboard, within minutes Thirsty had his new-found friend in hysterics by telling him that he was a perfectly harmless drunk who got his kicks out of floating around in the ocean at 6am impersonating King Neptune.

Thirsty and Mad Ivan settled into a couple of bottles of vodka, caught heaps more teraglin and headed for home just after daybreak only to run into the water police who had responded to Curly's 'man overboard' call and were searching the spot where he thought his mate had fallen in.

Thirsty got his fifteen minutes of fame and lapped it up. The press had a ball with him.

But the novelty wore off the day he threw up all over Mike Walsh on *The Midday Show* while telling the story for the millionth time.

He enjoyed the limelight so much that a couple of years later he tried the same stunt again.

Fair dinkum or staged, no one will ever know, because this time he disappeared, and has never been seen since . . .

My Hero — Bob Dyer

All boys have heroes and mine was the late and great Bob Dyer. But unlike most other blokes I was fortunate enough to meet and even fish with my hero, who made an everlasting impression on my fishing career and my life.

My childhood hero was Bob Dyer. That was back in the '50s and '60s, when Bob ruled Australian radio and TV and his show *Pick A Box* was about the biggest thing to hit this country since Mo and Stiffy. But while I admired Bob's on-air antics, it was his ability with a fishing rod and reel that really endeared him to me. I kept all the press-clippings about his giant catches, sat mesmerised at the newsreels and wished that one day I could be just like him and roam the waterways of the world in search of giant sea creatures.

Bob's best publicity came from the huge catches of sharks that he took out of Brisbane's Moreton Bay in the '50s, when he and his crew would head out to Yellow Patch on a Friday night in Bob's 11-metre *Tennessee* and return late Sunday afternoon towing about a dozen or so whalers, tigers and white pointers for all the public to gawk over.

And the sharks were huge. Nothing under 400 kilograms, and some of the white pointers were as big as 1000 kilograms and five metres long. The fans would gather in their thousands at the weigh station and Bob made the most of it, hamming it up in front of the cameras and telling the adoring public tales of how the savage man-eating beasts had attacked the boat in their feeding frenzy and how he and his crew were lucky to escape with their lives.

That was back in the days when the world was ignorant, and what we now know to be beautiful sea creatures — such as whales, dolphins and sharks — were considered dangerous monsters that must be killed and put to man's best use.

On the way out to his chosen fishing ground, Bob would call in at the Moreton Bay whaling station and pick up as much whale oil, blood and blubber as his boat could carry.

Once they were anchored up, the crew would berley with the whale offal and the sharks would cruise in their thousands for a snack. Bob was a huge man, and contrary to popular belief, he took his fishing deadly seriously; he was one of the world's truly great anglers.

Having selected which shark he would like to catch, Bob would feed it a bait attached to a heavy wire trace, set the hook and the battle would rage — sometimes for many hours at a time. But not all of the sharks that were hooked were landed. One of Bob's crewmen, Jack Farrell, whom I fished with many times in later years, told me amazing stories of breathtaking danger at the side of the boat.

'The big whites and the tigers were the worst,' he told me. 'It was alright for Bob to get all the glory at the weigh station but it was us poor buggers on the gaffs and with the tail-ropes that nearly got killed. The most awful trait of the tigers and whites is that they roll up in the gaff ropes — sort of like a huge, snapping aquatic yoyo, and the more they twist and lunge in the ropes, the closer they get to actually coming into the boat with us.'

'And don't ever let anyone tell you that sharks aren't agile and quick,' he would go on.

'With their torsos and tails wrapped up in the ropes, their huge heads would appear from nowhere over the side and they'd come at us in mid-air, biting and growling and lunging at anything in their way. I nearly got my head bitten off a hundred times by sharks with mouths the size of 44-gallon drums. It was a living nightmare.

'A lot of those huge sharks were just too big to handle and they escaped by sheer brute force as they smashed the gaffs, ropes and the boat. We weighed a lot of world records, but every white pointer, tiger and whaler shark record in the world is still swimming around out there somewhere after having escaped from us.'

My friend Jack is gone now and so is Bob, and, fortunately, so are those barbaric times when killing giant sea creatures was called adventure and the men who did it were called heroes. It was even legal way back then to harpoon dolphins and use them as berley and bait. This has long been outlawed, as has the use of mammal offal as berley.

But we didn't see it as barbaric. To me, my hero, Bob Dyer, was a great man who just did what few other men were game to do and few ever did.

As I grew older and my fishing preferences changed from beach fishing to rock fishing and then boat fishing, I eventually got to be a deckhand on a game-fishing boat out of Sydney, and one day at the Sydney Game Fishing Club I was introduced to Bob Dyer. I couldn't believe it. There I was shaking hands with the Great Man himself.

My skipper knew that I idolised Bob and said to him, 'Paul's our bilge rat. He's just started at the bottom in game fishing, Bob. Have you got a bit of advice for him?'

My hero towered over me, squeezed my hand in his huge mitt and said, 'I certainly have, young fella. Always remember that a man's boat is his castle and that you are a guest. Always leave it as you find it. Scrub the decks hard and don't leave a trace of the day's activities. That way you'll always be welcome. Some day you will be welcome on my boat.'

Little did he realise just how true those words would be. I couldn't wait to get home that night to ring my Mum in Perth and tell her I'd actually met Bob Dyer.

Through hard work and leaving people's boats as I found them, I eventually wound up as fishing master on Keith Whitehead's magnificent 11-metre Bertram, *Splashdown.* Keith was a three-time Olympian, having represented Australia in water polo. He was also a great friend of Bob Dyer, whom he called 'Pappy' because Bob had grown a big white beard. We used to bump into Bob from time to time and I got to say hello, but of course he never remembered me and I never reminded him of our brief encounter.

Through all of that time Bob never did or said anything to shatter my elusion of him. He was always the man that I had imagined him to be. He was polite and charming with the ladies, never got drunk and disgraced himself, was modest, and always in demand as an after-dinner speaker at game-fishing presentation nights. I was very proud that Bob Dyer said hello to me and that he was my hero.

And then one day when we were having a lay-day on *Splashdown* at Greenwell Point south of Sydney, and Bob Dyer's 16-metre *Blue Rhapsody* was tied up at the wharf beside us, Bob walked up to the bow of his boat and suggested to Keith that seeing as he (Keith) wasn't going fishing that day, maybe the 'young bloke' might like to go out fishing with him for the day.

Go fishing with Bob Dyer? I couldn't believe my ears. But it *was* true and I didn't have to be asked twice. And what a day it was. Bob released a small marlin he caught on light tackle and I got to see in real life just what a great angler he was. And when the day was over and *Blue Rhapsody* was tied up at the wharf, our team from *Splashdown* joined Bob and his crew for drinks and we all sat around and chatted and encouraged Bob to talk about the old days.

And when he did talk of those bygone days when the men who went to sea to kill giant sea creatures were heroes to a nation, he spoke with much sadness and regret that he had taken the lives of so many living things. He spoke of their gallantry in trying to escape, their terror as they lunged in the gaff ropes at his crew and their distress as they died a slow death tied up by their tails to the back of a boat.

He wondered if they felt humiliation as they were strung up on the gantry like murderers in the Dark Ages. He pondered the fact that they died only because they were hungry. In the last 15 years of his life, Bob Dyer never killed another living thing unless it was for the table.

And he preached to others about the foolishness of wanton destruction of living creatures. And they listened. And now more than 90 per cent of fish caught in game-fishing competitions, including sharks, are released to fight another day.

I am very pleased that Bob Dyer was my hero. For more reasons than one.

The Topless Shark

In the 1970s and '80s, the fishing team of Pam Hudspeth and Jack Farrell was one of the most successful this country has ever seen. Between them they rewote the game-fishing record books and to this day Pam holds more records than any other lady angler. Jack passed away in 1991. Pam has retired and breeds dogs in South Australia.

Prospects for shark fishing didn't look too bright that first Sunday in November as Pam Hudspeth and Jack Farrell headed northeast from Sydney Heads towards Long Reef.

Their discussion was not of how many fish they would catch but how long it would be before the elements would drive them back to the comforts of the Rose Bay marina. The 15 to 20 knot nor'-easter made for unpleasant conditions aboard Pam's 7.5-metre *Winamee II.*

Mooring up at Long Reef was not without its hazards either; the raging three-knot current from the north to the south and the jogging, choppy conditions combined to make the task much tougher than usual.

With the reef pick securely fastened, Jack and Pam set about preparing rigs for sharks and kingfish.

There's never much doing off Sydney in November so they decided to fish with light line to get as much sport as possible from the few-and-far-between predators. A rod and reel fitted with 15 kilogram test line was baited with a three kilogram kingfish and lowered to the bottom. It was intended for a shark.

The other baits of live yellowtail were set just below the surface on floats in the hope that they'd lure a migratory yellowfin tuna, though that was unlikely as the current had brought with it the customary pea soup-coloured water, which was not to the liking of surface species such as the predatory marlin and tunas.

BOTTOMLESS
KINGY
©REB 97

By mid-morning they had company, in the shape of Jack Paton, aboard his boat *Signa*, but as the conditions deteriorated, Jack decided to move *Signa* in closer to the coast, hopeful of a feed of snapper.

By 11am Jack and Pam were just about ready to call it a day when the ratchet on the 15 kilogram outfit went off, indicating something was interested in the kingie bait suspended just above the bottom. It was agreed that Jack was to take first strike of the day, so with the rod butt secured in the gimbaled-waist rod bucket, he wound up the clutch and struck hard, hoping the hook would penetrate deeply into the mouth of whatever had taken the bait.

Anticipating a docile old reef-dwelling grey nurse shark, Jack was surprised when the fish peeled line from the reel as if it didn't like the hook one bit and was heading for New Zealand.

Jack knuckled down to the fight, and after about 20 minutes, he was able to turn the fish and bring it to within about 15 metres of the boat . . . close, but still not close enough to identify it.

Jack tightened the drag to the limit, but the added strain only caused the fish to start circling the boat.

After several hair-raising trips to the bow of the boat to pass the rod and reel between the mooring rope and the vessel, Pam clambered up the flying bridge to get a better look at their adversary.

'It's a tiger, Jack,' she called, 'and it's a big 'un.'

This suprised both Jack and Pam. Tiger sharks off Sydney were not rare, but they certainly were unusual this early in the season, and they both knew that you could never tell whether these out-of-season fish were really early arrivals or leftovers from the previous season.

Still the circling continued . . . two hours of agonising, back-breaking angling. During that time Jack must have walked around the moored boat at least 20 times, each time having to pass the rod and reel under the anchor rope, which added to the physical torture.

Through all this the shark ventured no further than 45 metres from the boat. At last they decided they were in a no-win situation. They elected to 'throw the danbuoy', and go to the fish, rather than persist in trying to bring it to the boat on such light line.

'Throwing the danbuoy' consists of finding a shackled joint further

back on your anchor rope, disconnecting it, shackling a brightly coloured danbuoy to it and throwing the whole lot over the side. This enables the boat to leave the mooring, chase the fish and come back at a later date and pick the anchor rope up again.

It was almost as though the fish knew the chase was on — it headed east at breakneck speed with Jack and Pam churning through the rough seas in hot pursuit. It took an hour for the pursuit tactics to pay off; at last the big fish appeared on the surface, with the wire trace almost within reach.

Had they had another hand on the boat, that shark would have been theirs there and then. But Jack couldn't hold the fish in position long enough for Pam to come down from the flying bridge where she had to drive the boat, and take a wrap on the wire.

They had to watch as the shark took off again, undoubtedly shaken by being so close to the boat. Fifty, 100, then 200 metres of line disappeared from the reel as once again Pam headed the boat after their quarry.

Now they had time to get their bearings. They were about five kilometres south of their original position, and just off Sydney Heads.

Then an extraordinary thing happened. The tiger showed a complete reversal of form by turning a quick 180 degrees and making a beeline directly for North Head, or, to be more precise, straight toward Sydney Harbour. This suited Jack and Pam down to the ground as the nasty conditions were behind them now and the only bit of discomfort was when they would occasionally turn side-on to get a better angle at the fish.

As they approached North Head they were joined by *Signa*, who stayed close by for an hour before proceeding into the Watsons Bay weigh station to let them know that *Winamee II* was onto a good fish and to have the scales in readiness should all go well. *Signa* also arranged radio contact with them every hour on the hour. Now that they were organised, they could relax a little . . . or so they thought.

As *Winamee II* came closer to the cliffs, the backwash of the waves started to toss the boat about vigorously. Jack had to use all his skill to prevent a bust-off. Still on almost full drag, Jack couldn't get that fish any closer to the boat than about six metres.

And if they thought they had troubles before, they had no idea what was ahead. There was a raging flood tide, from recent heavy rains, forcing its way down Sydney Harbour and out to sea and its wake was forcing the boat back to the east. Now the tiger was 'bogging' into the flood tide, in typical tiger shark fashion — nosing into a fast current is their natural instinct.

To add further to their woes, the shark was heading straight for the shipping lanes at an incredible speed, and today, with the sun shining, the harbour was, of course, a hive of activity. First a pleasure cruiser, then a Japanese long-line tuna boat and then, believe it or not, a submarine, came within spitting distance of cutting the line.

To add to this already comical situation, they had to put up with sirens blaring and hooters hooting; some of them well-wishers, but most of them irate skippers who were forced off course by *Winamee II* as Jack and Pam manoeuvred this way and that trying to get a gaff shot at the fish.

What the hell! Pam did her job and navigated that whole amazing act right through the middle of the flotilla and toward Camp Cove, which, at the time, was Australia's most famous topless bathing beach. Camp Cove is on the foreshores of Sydney Harbour, just inside South Head.

So there they were. The world's unluckiest shark navigating the boat toward a topless beach, followed by a fleet of onlookers.

As *Winamee II* approached the beach it became obvious to the semi-nude bathers that this was no bream the lady and man on board were fighting. No way. No matter how you looked at it, the gripping drama going on in front of them was with a big fish.

And so, with much shrieking and boob-clutching, there was a mass exodus from the water onto the beach of scantily-clad beauties, much to the delight of the male onlookers who flocked to Camp Cove each weekend.

About now the shark started to ease down, and Jack felt the last of the line slip through his fingers and onto the reel. He shouted to Pam to leave the boat slowly idling ahead while he grabbed the wire trace in one hand and held onto the rod and reel with the other, thus enabling Pam to get the huge flying head gaff into the fish and secure the fish to the boat.

Pam's first hit with the big flyer was perfectly placed in the tougher section of the fish's underbelly near the gill cage. If there's anything on earth that can take your mind off bouncing boobs it's a 30 centimetre flying gaff stuck in your mid-section.

When the gaff went in it was as if a depth charge had been exploded beneath the boat — the shark expressed its disapproval by going berserk, snapping and kicking shit out of the transom of *Winamee II.*

The crowd was transfixed as another flyer went in and the shark tried to eat the marlin board and decapitate Jack with its flaying tail. Not a nipple moved from the beach until the tail rope was secured. Amid much jubilation, our heroes headed for the weigh station at Watsons Bay, waving to the crowd as they went.

The six-hour ordeal was over. Well, for Jack and Pam, at least.

To this day, some of those topless ladies are still convinced that that huge fish was hooked right where they saw it gaffed. And mothers always talk to their daughters. That's why, to this day, you rarely see the nubiles venture far out into the water at Camp Cove, for fear of being eaten by the friends of what became known as 'the topless shark'.

A Grand Tale

Anglers from all over the world come to Cairns each year to catch giant marlin with beaks like baseball bats and eyes the size of bread and butter plates. But few of these anglers intend to kill the fish, rather choosing to release it unharmed after the fight. One angler, however, did intend to take a monster marlin and mount it in his den. I went along for the ride and it was my job to kill it . . .

It was a big fish. No, not big — huge. If it wasn't for its one-metre sickle tail slicing the water about five metres back from the bait, we probably wouldn't have known it was there as we were trolling 'blind' with the sun glaring on the water.

But it was there, and judging by the way it was crawling all over our scad, we were in for some hot action.

I looked at the world's best black marlin skipper for a second opinion.

'She's a horse,' he mumbled. 'Hope the bastard eats.' It did. And if we got it alongside the boat, it was my job to kill it.

I was crewing on a special charter out of Cairns with the world-famous black marlin skipper, Captain Dennis 'Brazakka' Wallace. I had met and fished with Brazakka 25 years earlier in a Cairns light-tackle tournament and we had become good friends. Legend has it that he was raised by the local natives and his nickname is Aboriginal for 'wild man'. I never bothered to find out any more; that version suited me just fine.

We maintained our friendship over the years while pursuing our fishing careers, although those went in different directions. I chose to write about my passion, while Brazakka went on to become one of the greatest black marlin skippers on earth.

In a career spanning 25 years, he has captured or tagged and released thousands of black marlin, including more than 100 of these mightiest of all warriors that weighed in excess of the benchmark 1000 pounds.

Brazakka chartered for and became like a son to the late Lee Marvin. Over 12 seasons they weighed 13 granders and tagged at least a dozen more that would have made it. One was a bewildering 1320-pounder. That's a lot of sashimi!

Brazakka and I kept in touch, and whenever I was in Cairns or he was in Sydney, we'd get together for a beer. So it came as no great surprise when he rang and asked if I'd like to spend 10 days with him out on the Great Barrier Reef during peak marlin time. Of course I would! But what's the catch?

Seeing as he hadn't killed a marlin in eight years and he required the services of only one deckhand to let them go, he was in a spot.

His charter, a Texan, wanted to take a big fish. He had fished with Brazakka for five seasons and had released hundreds of fish, including a few that would have been more than a grand. This season he wanted to kill one and have it mounted on his wall.

He figured that if the Japanese long-liners could take 800 000 assorted billfish out of the ocean each year, then his one fish wasn't going to have a dramatic effect on their decline.

As Brazakka's deckie would be pretty busy holding the huge fish on the wire leader as it was brought within range of a gaff, they would need a second man to perform the coup de grâce. I would be that second man.

This moment of mayhem is the most dangerous part of the saga, and is known as 'the kill'. This is when bones are broken, reputations smashed, and wire and gaff men are often dragged over the side. I've gaffed tiger and mako sharks up to 800 pounds, and they are a handful, but the biggest marlin I've gaffed would be no bigger than 300 pounds.

But I'm a notorious boat slut who would do anything for a ride, let alone 10 days out on the Reef. I accepted immediately, knowing there was the slim possibility that they might not catch a whopper and my services wouldn't be required.

I could just snap away with my camera, get lots of stories and classic pics and live it up at night on the mothership. Yes, I'd love to go to Cairns.

Actually the term 'fishing at Cairns' is a myth. 'Fishing out of Cairns' would be more accurate. An expatriate Yank, George Bransford, put Cairns on the map in late 1966 with Richard Obach's 1064 pound black marlin taken on an 80 pound breaking-strain line — the first grander taken anywhere in the world since Cabo Blanco in Peru in the early '50s, and the first thousand pounder ever taken on 80 pound line. Bransford's tiny *Sea Baby I* represented half of the Cairns game-fishing fleet then.

They would daytrip the 30-odd miles out to the Reef at an agonizingly slow 10 to 12 knots, punching into a southeast trade wind. They would return with their fish at night and weigh them on the huge scales at the end of the marlin wharf for all to see.

This restricted Bransford to the reefs adjacent to Cairns — either Jennie Louise or Euston. Here the continental shelf drops off into a bottomless abyss and the water changes colour from a pissy green to inky onyx in a matter of metres.

It is in this warm water that the giant female black marlin congregate between August and November each year to lay their eggs, and the smaller males, fish up to 350 pounds (160 kilograms), are in hot pursuit to fertilise them, leading to this spawning period being labelled the 'hot bite'.

Why the black marlin choose this area alone to spawn remains a mystery. Perhaps it is the abundance of bait fish along the continental shelf, the rich vegetation and crustacean-encrusted wall that runs the length of Australia's eastern seaboard.

The huge schools of bait fish such as scad, tuna, mahi-mahi, mackerel, wahoo and rainbow runners attract the giant fish thus creating by far the best black marlin fishing grounds in the world. More thousand-pound fish are caught here in a week than in all of the world's other hot spots combined for a year.

And so, as word of Bransford's extraordinary catch spread, more charter boats and anglers flocked to the area, captures increased and the sportfishing fleet grew as captains looked further afield for the big fish. Among other unfished areas, their travels took them to the Ribbon Reefs that stretch from well north of Cairns to Lizard Island (about 100 miles up the track).

And to work their way north, fishing the Ribbons as they went, required a decent-sized live-aboard boat to accommodate cook, anglers and crew. As most of the fishing boats were smaller, quicker and more manoeuverable, motherships, which could take up to three boats and their occupants at a time, were built. They would meander up the coast inside the reef, and have dinner and a cold drink waiting for the day-boats at the end of a hard day's fishing.

Soon it became impractical to go back to Cairns at all. Day-boats would go out and stay out for three months at a time, living and refuelling off the motherships and flying their anglers out by float plane — yet another business that developed to cater for the demands of the ever-increasing marlin fleet.

My home for the 10 days was the 120-foot *Achilles II,* the largest mothership in the fleet, with a replacement value of around $12 million. Sitting like a satellite city inside the No. 5 Ribbon Reef, it made our 40-foot day-boat, *Reel Affair,* look like a dingy. Still, at upwards of $2000 a day each for up to three boats at a time, you would expect the ultimate. As we were the only boat living on it at the time, we had the *Achilles II* and its doting crew all to ourselves.

As I arrived by float plane, Brazakka was waiting on the back of *Achilles II* to meet me.

'Say hello to Big Bill from Texas,' he said as he introduced us. Bill was a giant of a man, with shoulders like a padded-up gridiron player.

'How y'all doin'?' he grinned as he plonked his mitt around mine and shook it until my whole body ached. 'Brazakka tells me you're gonna gaff that big fish for me. It don't worry ya none, does it? Killin' one of 'em, ah mean?'

'No, not at all,' I replied. 'That's what I'm here for.'

'Good,' he exclaimed. 'Me and my darlin' Connie have been comin' down here these past five years and I reckon it's time for me to take one big 'un.'

And so off we went — no time to unpack, just load the gear into the cabin and take off fishing.

Under normal circumstances I would be disappointed to go home after a day's fishing. But getting back to the *Achilles* at night was a real treat — a chilled beer, fabulous food and a chat about the day's events. And there was plenty to talk about. The first couple of days were good, with a few fish up to 400 pounds released. The fourth day was one of the best fishing days of my life. We were fishing off the No. 10 Ribbon and the bite was hot. We got 10 fish up, six of them bit, and we hooked up and released four. The biggest was around 800 pounds — a whopper by my standards, but only a tiddler compared with what was to come.

It was on the fifth day that Mrs Huge appeared behind the baits. She was lit up like a firecracker, her pectorals a stark white and her barrel torso a myriad of fluorescent blue-and-white bars, something that they do when they are about to eat or mate. Brazakka turned the boat out of the sun so he could get a better look at the fish.

'Big bastard,' he mumbled. That's about as excited as he got. He normally loves a chat, but not when the bite's on.

She took the bait and Brazakka gunned the boat ahead and hooked up. *Reel Affair* went nose first into the five-metre swell, with the huge marlin peeling off the 130 pound line (against 60 pounds of clutch pressure) as if it was a roll of toilet paper. Big Bill had his work cut out just getting the rod from the gunwale to the chair unaided.

At last he was settled and Mark the deckie buckled him up to the harness. Only now did I see why the big Southerner was held in such esteem for his angling ability. His powerful legs and back combined to put pressure against the fish and gain line at every opportunity. But as much as the Texan took, the big fish took it back.

The acrobatics were spectacular. How anything as big as that could propel itself clear of the water was beyond me. 'How big?' I asked Brazakka. 'Between thirteen and fourteen hundred,' he growled, and he'd know.

I stayed out of the way on the flying bridge. My gaffs were ready in the cockpit, secured to the stem of the fighting chair. Soon I would have to earn my keep.

And so the fight continued, fortunately on or near the surface, away from the sharks. Then she didn't jump anymore. She just bogged down into the current about 18 metres below the surface, with Brazakka full speed in reverse after her.

Two hours later, Big Bill was still holding up pretty well. He could still manage a huge grin. 'This is the hardest fish I ever fought,' he cussed. 'She just don't wanna die.'

After two-and-a-half hours, it was time. The trace was up and Mark took a wrap in his heavily gloved hands and lifted the mammoth fish toward the boat. I was beside him with my gaff ready. 'Don't choke,' he said. 'Just a neat shot in the shoulder.'

By now all five metres of the giant fish was coming. I was mesmerised by the sheer size of it as its head — with its beak like a baseball bat and an eye the size of a bread and butter plate — broke the surface in an attempt to leap about five metres from the boat.

Until my dying breath I will never forget the look of defiance in her giant eye. It was ablaze with fear, and my reflection seemed to disappear deep into it as I prepared to kill her. She was tired from the fight. Brazakka inched the boat back and Mark took bigger wraps on the trace. It was almost time for the kill.

I readied my gaff. Another few inches and I would impale her to the boat and she would die. So close now.

The water was pouring into the cockpit as we reversed into the sea. And now she was alongside, perfectly positioned for me to perform my duty, I steadied . . .

'No,' called the big Texan. 'Cut her loose.'

'What the . . .' I yelled. 'She's here.'

'Don't argue,' he commanded. 'Let her go.'

Mark cut the wire and the huge fish swam off into the abyss. I was dumbfounded. I turned to the big Texan, who was smiling. Nothing was said. It wasn't necessary.

I looked up at the world's greatest black marlin skipper and he was smiling too.

The Revenge of the Giant Mullet

Most people dream of catching a giant fish but to this old fishing writer it's all too hard; I'd rather just go along for the ride, have a cold beer and photograph the action. But every so often I get conned into doing a bit of work . . .

I don't catch many fish these days. I'm too old and too lazy. My idea of a great day's fishing is handlining out of a boat for snapper over a cold tinny and shootin' the breeze with the boys. And if I don't catch a fish, who cares. It's the day that counts.

That's why I love my adventures out of Cairns with my old mate Captain Dennis 'Brazakka' Wallace, the world-famous Aussie game charter-boat skipper. I ride along with him for 10 days or so each year and get pictures and stories of the giant black marlin they catch. And if I want to, I can do a bit of handlining for red emperor or coral trout.

Thanks to Brazakka, I've hobnobbed with a multibillionaire from Arkansas, knights of the realm, legendary golfers and the rich and famous from all over the world. Not bad for a kid who ran away to sea at 14 and could hardly read or write. Fishing has been very kind to me, but that doesn't mean that I have to actually catch those giant fish any more.

Leave me out of that backbreaking stuff where I sit in the game chair for hours on end. Been there, done that. These days I'm happy to ride along and let the paying customers do all that while I get a sweat up taking pictures and writing stories about them.

A couple of years back, Brazakka was fishing his boat for the season, the 14.5-metre *Kestelle,* at Opal Reef, about 110 kilometres northeast of Cairns, and had arranged a lift for me out to her on a Cairns-based

10-metre Bertram named *Chamois Free*, skippered by hot-shot Miami captain John Phillips and crewed by deckie John (Foxy) Fox.

'You'll have a good time with the boys,' Brazakka had told me. 'Just meet 'em on the wharf and load all your gear on, open a cold beer and they'll have you out here with me in a few hours, give or take catching a few marlin along the way.' It sounded all right to me.

The boys call their spasmodic trips out to the game-fishing fleet the 'mail run'. They troll baits and lures for giant marlin all the way, then deliver any letters, spare parts or urgent supplies to the crews, stay on the boat overnight and fish all the way home the following day. There isn't a mailman on earth who wouldn't murder for a job like that.

After introducing myself to Captain JP and the Fox and as we pulled out from the Cairns wharf, I was introduced to Ken Newton, a veterinarian from Miami, who was holidaying in Australia for the first time with his wife and baby son.

'So you're our angler for the day,' I assumed of the dog-doctor. 'It looks good out there so you might catch yourself a giant marlin.'

'No way,' he replied. 'I wouldn't know how to catch one of those if my life depended on it. They told me this fishing photojournalist was coming up from Sydney to do a story and that he was going to catch all of the fish. I assume they meant you.'

I was trapped. The swines had got me nicely. Brazakka had obviously told them I was bone-idle and that it was time I got a solid workout. I tried to escape but it was too late. The boat was well on its way and there was no turning back. It was too far to swim and I couldn't insult my host. I had to pray they didn't hook anything huge.

But who was the other bloke, the Yank? How did he fit into the act? 'Are you a friend of JP's from the States?' I asked.

'Never met him before in my life,' he replied.

I was intrigued. 'Are you a paying customer then?' I asked, knowing it was a stupid question because if he was, then why was I going to catch all the marlin?

'Quite the opposite,' he replied. 'These guys are paying me $50 to come out for a couple of days. This morning I was on my way to the tourist agency at the end of the wharf to make inquiries to take my wife and baby son to see the koalas and kangaroos for the day, when I stopped to look at his boat and he asked me if I'd like to ride out overnight because they had this mad journalist coming out and if they hooked into a monster marlin, they were a crewman short. My wife said it was too good an opportunity to miss, so here I am.'

I couldn't believe my ears. One minute this guy was walking down the wharf to get tickets for the full-on family tourist trip, the next he was on his way out into the most prolific marlin waters in the world for a couple of days — and he was getting paid for it! Truth is stranger than fiction.

'JP's determined to get you a fish,' Foxy told me as he handed me earplugs to overcome the roar of the diesels as we headed east.

'*Chamois Free* raises more marlin than any other boat in the fleet and he'd love you to see how we do it so you can get some pictures and maybe do a story about us and the boat. He loves this old girl more than anything in the world. We're going to troll lures first and then I'm going to put out a special bait that I've been saving just for you. It's guaranteed to get us a giant marlin. Get a load of this.'

With that he went to the icebox and produced the biggest mullet that I'd ever seen in my life. I went green as I looked at it in horror. It must have been a metre long and it was already rigged with a giant hook in its head and a wire trace to be trolled behind the boat to catch a monster marlin.

Now I've spent the best part of a lifetime maligning mullet — over the years I have written countless stories about how rotten they are to eat and how even my cats wouldn't eat one even though they would eat their own young if given the chance. I've had a ball at the poor old mullet's expense. Every time I was short of a story idea I'd just drop another bucket full on the mullet and the readers would lap it up.

And now here was a giant mullet sent to haunt me. Horror of horrors! The revenge of the giant mullet! I vowed there and then I would never again say anything horrid about mullet. But was it too late? I was about to find out.

Fox put his prize bait back on ice. No sooner were the lures in the water than we hooked into a little black marlin of about 90 kilograms and I had it tagged and released in about five minutes.

Needless to say, the American vet was almost comatose with excitement as he watched that marlin jump all over the ocean, having never seen anything like it before in his life. I remember thinking at the time; 'What's this joker going to be like if we hook a whopper?'

Then it was time to back off on the revs, put out the baits, cruise leisurely north and try and hook Mrs Huge (all giant marlin are females). With a bit of luck we wouldn't, and I could sit back in the tropical sun and chew on a cold one.

But that was not to be and the giant mullet bait was only in the water five minutes when a big black marlin cruised up to it and swallowed it just the way my kid scoffs down a Big Mac. Whooshka! It was off at a million miles an hour, pounding across the surface and peeling line from the reel as if it were cotton from a bobbin.

I tried to convince JP that seeing as I had already caught one fish, maybe our new chum, the vet, should take this strike. 'Are you serious?' JP yelled from the tuna tower. 'He's in no condition to talk, let alone fight a fish. Just get a load of him.' I looked at the Yank, who by this stage had his frothing tongue hanging loosely from the corner of his mouth. He was so delirious with excitement that all he could do was point at the fish and mouth the words 'Did you see that?' or something to that effect.

I somehow got the huge rod and reel out of the rod holder and staggered with it to the chair, without being dragged over the side. Once harnessed in, I put my full weight on the fish and realised that I was going to be there for a while. After about 15 minutes my back felt broken, my arms were ready to drop off and my legs had turned to boiled spaghetti.

The Yank was rapidly approaching dementia and was a walk-up-start for the rubber room at the Betty Ford Clinic when, and if, he ever went home.

After an hour I'd had enough. Fortunately, so had the fish. According to Foxy it was about three metres long and would have weighed about 250 kilograms . He took the trace and held the subdued marlin alongside the boat while I wobbled out of the chair and put a capture tag in it and let it go while the Yank leaned over the side, salivating and drooling at its size.

We cooled off with a beer and the boys dropped me off at Brazakka's boat an hour later and tied up alongside for the night. The last I saw of the Yank for the day, he was full of Bundy and Coke and falling about on the back of *Chamois Free* as the boys knocked him up an Aussie steak on the boat's barbie.

The following morning he was heard shrieking over a breakfast tinnie, 'How long's this been going on?' as they headed back in the general direction of Cairns. We heard later on the two-way that JP and Foxy put the poor wretch into an 1100 pound marlin that mercifully jumped off after a titanic four-hour battle.

And me? I couldn't walk or move a muscle for a couple of days. Almost wrecked my holiday. I'll never say anything bad about a mullet again.

Tacklin' Tassie's Tuna

Of all of the fishin' holes in Australia, Tasmania takes a lot of beating. It's got the scenery, and the fish — and the Taswegians are a delight . . . nothing seems to faze them in the least. And, incredibly, that includes their extraordinary weather, which can be bitter one minute and boiling the next. And the rougher it gets . . . the more they like their fishing . . .

They've got a saying in southeast Tasmania that goes like this: 'Tassie has four distinct seasons. Trouble is, you get 'em all in one day.'

I was invited down to Tassie a couple of years back to do a story on the Australian Bluefin Tuna Championships, put on by the Tuna Club of Tasmania, and believe me, the locals fish in mountainous seas and winds that are a knot or two short of an eight on the Richter scale.

Then, in the twinkling of an eye, the sun's out, the wind drops and the seas flatten to millpond conditions. I put my head down for a short nap once, in the middle of a howling gale, and woke up a few minutes later in perfect conditions, wondering if I hadn't dreamt it all. It was a weird experience. The locals take it all in their stride, though, and reckon 'city folk' like me will never get used to it. They're dead right.

But weird fishing conditions or not, I wouldn't miss an opportunity to fish Tassie, because what some spots might lack in fish, they certainly make up for in scenery — and hospitality that's darn near impossible to beat.

Forget all that rubbish about Taswegians having two heads and being a bunch of country hicks. That may apply in some areas, the same as it does up here on the mainland, but for my money the Tasmanians are the friendliest and most hospitable people you're ever likely to meet.

C'MON KIDD! IT'S A PERFECT DAY...

So when Ron Di Felice from Tasmanian Tourism rang and asked if I'd like to be their guest at the Bluefin Championships, I didn't hesitate. I'd never been blue-water fishing in Tassie before, so the message on the bottom of Ronnie's fax — 'You will have a great time experiencing our crazy fishing style' — went straight over the top of my head. Boy, was I in for a giant surprise.

The competition is held out of Eaglehawk Neck, a small fishing village about an hour's drive south of Hobart. Ron had arranged accommodation for me at the local hotel overlooking the glorious Pirate's Bay.

The following morning at 6am, I stuck my head out the window for a weather check and had my hair flattened by a breeze that was the equivalent of standing behind a jumbo jet on take off. 'They'll call it off,' I said to myself as I slid back into the warmth and pulled the doona over my head. My peace and quiet was short-lived.

'Come on, mate, they're all waiting for you at the wharf,' Ronnie called as he pounded on my door to wake me up. 'We'll get some tuna today for sure. The weather's perfect for it.'

Maybe I had been dreaming about the weather being so crook; I stuck my head out again for a second opinion. Ouch! It was like someone stabbing me in the face with a thousand frozen needles — the breeze had picked up to the speed needed to blow a sailor off your sister.

'You've brought the good weather with you,' Captain Gerald Spalding told me as he gunned his magnificent 17-metre Randall-hulled charter boat, the *Norseman III*, through a six metre wave.

'The last couple of days the weather's been lousy. The sun was out, there was hardly any breeze and the seas were as flat as a lizard drinkin'. We've been waitin' for this change. We need a little bit of activity on the surface to bring the bluefin up.'

A little bit of activity on the surface! As big and heavy as it was, *Norseman III* was all over the joint like a matchstick in a washing machine. I looked around for a bit of sympathy.

'Terrific conditions,' I said, as a joke, to Rob Richardson, one of our fishing team. 'Yeah, she's a beauty,' he replied. 'Looks like you brought the good weather with you. With a bit of luck, the wind might pick up a bit to gale force, but that's really asking too much.'

I'd died and gone to fisherman's hell. I looked around at the rest of the team: Rino De Santo, Paul Williams, Anthony Whitbread and deckie John Rooke. The 'Bottom End Boys', they call themselves. They were all grinning from ear to ear like a gang of carpet snakes that had just crawled out of a chicken house.

'Seein' as you're on board, Gerald's going to take us out to the continental shelf as a special treat,' John explained. 'And just before the shelf, there's a big hole about the size of a couple of football fields — on these good days the waves can get up to 10 metres in there.

'He must have taken an instant liking to you because he only takes special people to the hole, so act surprised when we hit it and let him tell you all about it himself. You'll know when we're there. The boat will nearly capsize when the first big greenie hits us.'

I couldn't wait. And to celebrate our journey into aquatic hell and back (I hoped!), my new chums offered me cold beers, pickled onions and spicy salami and cheese sambos. I thought I was going to throw up for the first time in 40 years of going to sea.

When I asked where the raft and life jackets were, they told me not to worry about them because if the boat sank she had a watertight compartment up front and it was better to cling to the nose of the boat, as it stuck out of the water, than try to make it to any nearby islands and be pounded to death on the rocks.

I was so pleased I'd asked.

We were in the hole, rising and falling about eight metres, when the first tuna struck. Our angler mercifully pulled the hooks and it escaped.

'Bloody shame we lost that fish,' Gerald cursed. 'I love backin' the boat up on them tuna in here in the hole on these good days. It gives the crew a chance to get a good look at the hull of the boat when she's right out of the water and let me know if it needs a clean or not.'

He seemed a little disappointed when I crashed on the divan just as we were passing through the second football field. When I awoke about an hour later, everything was different. It was eerie. I could actually hear the engine noises over the waves. In fact, there were no waves. The boat wasn't pitching and rolling, and the crew were dead silent. The wind and seas had been replaced by blinding rain and lightning. And the sun was shining.

Gerald was really pissed off. 'That bloody beaut weather was only a squall,' he grizzled. 'And now we're gettin' the lousy weather back, bugger it. Just look at it. Almost flat seas and the sun shining. At least we've got some rain and lightning on the way.'

Terrific. Imagine getting through the day without rain and lightning. What a bummer. All of the anglers also seemed depressed that the gale had subsided, and when we returned home fishless they prayed for 'good' weather the next day.

'We'll just have to make the most of it,' Ronnie complained when he picked me up at the hotel in the dark of the following morning. 'The winds will only be gusting up to about 40 knots, and the sea isn't going to get much better than a four-metre swell.'

Gerald was a little more enthusiastic. 'Great day for showin' you around,' he said as *Norseman III* broached under a side-on five-metre wall of green water a few minutes after we left the wharf at Fortescue Bay. He pointed knowingly at a giant rock formation sticking out of the ocean ahead of us like Cleopatra's Needle.

'That's the Big Hippolite,' he enthused. 'On a good tuna day the waves break over the top of her and you can't see her at all.' I couldn't wait to get out there on a good tuna day. The Big Hippolite was at least 30 metres tall.

As our next sightseeing spot was Tasman Island, a few miles to the south, we had the wind, rain, fog patches and huge waves coming at us side-on while we trolled half-a-dozen lures through the thick of it. Most of the lures spent more time out of the water than in it.

And just when I was feeling crook for the second time in 40 years of going to sea, we got a solid strike. The boys got their rods in and out of the road and let Ronnie play what was obviously a big and powerful fish.

After a 15-minute battle on 15 kilogram line, Ronnie had the 25 kilogram tuna alongside and I got my first good look at what the

Japanese pay up to $200 a kilogram for to eat raw as sushi and sashimi.

And what a beautiful fish. Short, stocky and built like a guided missile. Designed to hunt and kill. The ultimate ocean warrior.

The boys were optimistic about catching more but all of a sudden the weather deteriorated something shocking; the wind dropped off, the sun came out and the seas abated to a leisurely swell.

'I must have run over a fuckin' Chinaman,' Gerald cursed. 'Just when I find the spot, the weather turns shithouse. Let's pray for some great weather tomorrow. In the meantime I'll show you Tasman Island, one of the highlights of the trip south.'

It was then I discovered why the Count of Monte Cristo chose the Chateau d'If — the other choice was Tasman Island! Its highlight, the lighthouse, must be the bleakest, most isolated, miserable place I've ever laid eyes on. It's worth the trip, but you wouldn't want to live there.

And so, with that one fish, and a couple the boys had caught the day before I arrived, *Norseman III* hit the front of the competition with a day to go. Could they hang on to win the most coveted trophy of them all: Champion Boat?

I didn't get much sleep that night because the wind was trying to rip the roof off the pub to let the torrential rain in. Good. They would cancel the day's fishing and my new friends would become Champion Boat. With yesterday's fish I had my story and pictures and everyone was happy. Finally my broken sleep was interrupted by Ronnie pounding on the door.

'Mate, let's get moving,' he yelled through the door. 'We've got the perfect tuna weather and Gerald's got the gun deckie comin' down all the way from northern Tassie. If you ever want to see some action, today's the day.'

I tried not to even contemplate what it was going to be like out in the boat. Just the drive to the wharf took an extra 10 minutes because we were driving into the wind. I tried to get out of going by explaining that I had a bad case of terminal dandruff, industrial fatigue and advanced fluff in the navel, but there was no way this lot were going to let me escape.

Gerald was drooling and salivating out of the corner of his mouth like Sir Les Patterson full of the turps. 'She's a bottler,' he enthused, rubbing his frozen hands together with glee. 'Perfect tuna weather. The wind's from the southeast at 50 knots and gusting to about 70. And the seas could be as high as 10 metres. You'll see it all today.'

As I fled up the gangplank in the direction of the hotel and my warm bed, Gerald grabbed me by my shirt collar, yanked me back on board and introduced me to the gun deckie from the north. 'Bert, say g'day to the fishin' and writin' photographic journalist from the mainland.

'Paul, Bert drove all through the night in blinding rain and fog to be here 'cause he can sniff a tuna day a million miles away. Can't you, Bert? And he's gunna get us a bunch of 'em for your story.'

Bert shook my hand vigorously. The huge toothless smile through the red beard that covered most of his face said it all.

Today was indeed a tuna day.

As we rounded the corner it was like staring death straight in the face. It was like the end of the world. Armageddon. The conflict of the forces of good and evil on the battlefield of the Apocalypse. The sky was black and the rain pounded huge seas that had been whipped up by the gale-force winds.

And the tuna? The boys caught three whoppers up to 30 kilograms and lost a couple more in the appalling conditions. The gun deckie from the north was pretty to watch and the boys took out Champion Boat, Champion Team and a swag of other goodies.

And me? I closed my eyes under the shower that night and fell over. Would I do it again? As much as I've complained, I'd have to say yes. A day out with the Bottom End Boys is worth the punishment.

From both the sea and from them.

'Women and Children First? Not Always.'

The unwritten law of the sea is that if a boat is sinking, be it a yacht, fishing boat or an ocean liner, no matter what, the women and children are to be rescued first. And that is usually the case . . . but there are exceptions to every rule . . .

I've been involved in several life-threatening situations involving sinking ships over the years, and no matter what the danger was to those on board the boat, it was always a case of women and children to be rescued first, even if this was at the cost of the lives of any of the men on board.

After all, that is the unwritten law of the sea. But is that always the case?

Apparently not – but more about that a little later.

Back in the early '70s I was a deckhand on a game-fishing boat out of Port Stephens on the northern NSW coast. We were heading back to port one afternoon when an unexpected squall hit from the south. The angry weather front was probably only a couple of miles wide but its cracking lightning, blinding rain and gusting winds of up to about 60 knots whipped the sea into a frenzy and created waves of up to 10 metres high.

And then it was gone, leaving us to almost surf in to Port Stephens on the giant waves it left in its wake. But others in smaller craft had been less fortunate. Between the headlands at the entrance to Port Stephens, the shallow water had created huge waves, and lots of small fishing boats had been caught unawares.

Those who were wise to the ways of the sea had seen the disaster

coming; they cut their anchor ropes and fled. Safer than pulling the anchor up and being caught in the horrendous seas and possibly killed.

As we steamed into the maelstrom we almost ran over a 6-metre cabin cruiser that was sinking before our eyes. The two men and one woman on board had put on life jackets in readiness for their anticipated swim, but I doubt they would have survived if we hadn't come along.

The waves that were breaking over them and their boat were huge, and by the time we got to them the boat had completely sunk, except for the bow, which was sticking about a metre out of the water. They were clinging to that.

All the men could think about was the safety of the woman. 'Save Gladys, save Gladys,' they called as our skipper manoeuvred the boat close enough to throw a line and drag them aboard without swamping them in the massive seas.

The men risked their lives by letting go of their boat and tying the rope around the lady, who, incredibly, seemed to be the calmest of them all.

Once secured to the lifeline, we dragged her to us and over the tuck of the boat to safety. Around her neck she had her handbag, which was the only thing she had time to grab before the boat sunk. That's woman's intuition for you.

Then we got the two blokes the same way. I've never forgotten how concerned they were for Gladys, who turned out to be one of the men's wives. There was no hesitation in getting her to safety first, even if it meant them drowning.

Another time I was with Jack and Signa Paton on their magnificent gameboat *Signa* when we came across an upturned cabin cruiser in the notorious shark fishing ground, The Peak, about six nautical miles off Sydney's Maroubra Beach. Four blokes clinging to its hull.

Jack immediately reported it to the Volunteer Coastal Patrol, a well-intentioned group of private individuals who were ever at the ready to assist the police in offshore rescues. Sadly, not all of the volunteers were very experienced in the ways of the sea and in lots of cases they were more of a hindrance than a help. For this reason the game-fishing boats referred to them as 'McHale's Navy'.

'Volunteer Coastal Patrol come in, over,' Jack called into the two-way radio.

'VCP, ten four, over,' came the instant reply, as if the bloke slept with the radio.

'This is *Signa* calling. We're out of radio range of Sydney Water Police and we've just rescued four blokes from an upturned boat at The Peak. Can you send someone out to salvage the boat, over.'

'Ten four *Signa*. On our way. Can you describe the boat?'

Jack frowned. 'Yes,' he replied. 'It's the only boat with a yellow hull floating upside down at The Peak . . . you imbecile.'

Then there was the time we were on our way down to the Sir John Young Banks off Nowra one summer's day. We came across a yacht that was sinking in dead calm seas after apparently striking a submerged object. Of the seven people on board, only the two children and the lady were wearing life jackets when we found them clinging to their half-inflated dinghy alongside the stricken yacht, about a mile offshore.

There was no question that the three life jackets they managed to grab as the yacht capsized should go to the kids and the lady. That's the law of the sea.

Special Constable John Whitehead, of the Sydney Water Police, tells me that they have never aided in a sea rescue where it has been anything but women and children first. That's the way it is in Australia, and, for that matter, most parts of the world. But not all.

The rule of the sea of 'women and children first' rather than 'every man for himself' seems to be as old as marining itself. And the other unwritten law of the sea was that the captain always went down with his ship, unless it was avoidable.

After a long voyage from England in 1878, the ill-fated passenger ship *Loch Ard* struck a reef off the Australian coast. After seeing that all who could reach safety had, Captain George Gibb gallantly went down with his ship in true British maritime tradition.

In 1852, when the troopship *HMS Birkenhead* struck a reef off South Africa, over 400 sailors and officers stood on deck and went down with their ship after the women and children had filled the only available lifeboats.

Whether or not a liner's orchestra can be considered crew is debatable. Yet the band struck up a ragtime tune as the *Titanic* sank, and they sank with her. Hence the Harry Chapin classic song *The Dance Band on The Titanic*, which prompted such classic lines as, 'The iceberg's on the starboard bow . . . won't you dance with me?'

The *Titanic*'s pursers shook hands with First Officer Lightoller (he survived), said 'Goodbye, old man', and went down with their ship. The *Titanic*'s Captain, Edward Smith, also sank with his ship. The last time Captain Smith was seen alive, he was saving a child.

Such acts of bravery are but a few in the long history of seafaring. But it doesn't always turn out that way. The sinking of the *Achille Lauro* in 1994 brought with it tales of cowardice and looting by the Italian and South American crew members and eyewitnesses reported them elbowing women and children out of the way to get to the lifeboats. Once there, there was no budging them. One officer even ripped off his uniform so he would look like a passenger.

Passengers complained that the *Achille Lauro*'s officers and crew showed little or no interest in the survival of passengers and when survivors were transferred to a rescue ship from the lifeboats, some of the crew were already on board, showered and in fresh clothes. So much for gallantry.

The Greek liner *Lakonia* sank off Madeira in 1963, taking with it 125 British passengers, due to what the official inquiry described as the 'gross negligence on carrying out procedures for abandoning ship' of the surviving captain and his crew.

But the classic of them all would have to be the captain of the *Oceanis*, which sank off South Africa in 1991, without loss of life. The captain was the first over the side, with many of his crew in hot pursuit, much to the bewilderment of the 380 passengers.

'I couldn't care less what people say about me,' he later stated. 'When I say "Abandon ship" that means everybody, and it doesn't matter who gets off first and that includes me. "Abandon" is for everyone.'

I wonder if he'd give his seat to a lady on a bus! Hardly.

Moreton and Luna Park

Fishing club yarns are usually true and I believe this story is, because I knew the characters involved. Mind you, the story has been told and re-told so many times over the years that it's hard to know what to believe . . . but who cares, as long as we get a good laugh!

Clem Brown had more nicknames than there are fleas on a cattle dog. 'Moreton Bay', 'Irish' and 'Rughead', to name but a few. All because he wore a hairpiece — more commonly known as a Moreton Bay Fig, an Irish Jig or a Rug.

And it was the most ordinary wig you could ever imagine. They say that once it fell off while he was walking through a cow paddock, and he tried on six before he found the right one.

To add to his woes, Moreton had the best pair of crossed eyes ever to gaze across a bar. 'Punters' eyes', we called 'em — one each way. They reckon that when he cried, the tears rolled down his back.

What with the wonky mince pies and the very detectable Irish, poor old Moreton didn't have much going for him. Which is probably why he joined our fishing club. Needless to say, he didn't have much luck with the ladies; that is, until he met our club's good-time girl, Cynthia 'Luna Park' Morts.

She loved us calling her Luna, believing it was because she was lots of laughs and fun to be with. The real reason was that all the blokes had been there at least once or twice.

When poor old Moreton clapped his crossed peepers on her it was love at first sight — on his part anyway.

We still reckon that the poor bastard was looking in her direction but actually seeing the plaster cast of 'Tight Lines' McKenzie's groper on the wall over his shoulder.

It was debatable who was the better sort, Luna or the groper, but Moreton pursued her with vigour. She tormented the poor bastard until his orchestra stalls felt like a bull terrier was hangin' off 'em. She accepted his come-ons but wouldn't let him touch her, let alone do the business.

That is, until the day we let the cat out of the bag and told her he was loaded, which was half-pie true. Of course he had to have a few bob. What could he spend it on? There wasn't a female alive who would go out with him, 'cos he was such a dud sort. He didn't smoke or gamble. They say that the only time he ever went to Randwick races he watched the horses go round and thought he was at Caulfield where they run in the opposite direction.

Every time the poor bastard had a beer he'd miss his mouth and pour it over his shoulder.

The strangest thing about the whole bizarre affair was that we couldn't convince Luna that he wore a wig.

'Bullshit,' she would say. 'You're just saying that to take the piss out of us. Besides, no one would be allowed to sell anything as bad as that. It has to be real. He just doesn't wash his hair very often.'

And of course he denied it was a rug. He even let her comb it and try and pull it off, falsely screaming in pain as she did so. And so the relationship developed. But she still wouldn't let him give her a Wellington boot.

The poor bastard was going nuts. In desperation he bought a beautiful boat, a 25-foot Bertram, and called it *Luna*. She was suitably impressed and went out fishing with him on the condition that someone else came along. Trapped on a boat all day with that horny, cross-eyed cane toad wasn't her idea of fun.

And so the courtship continued until she decided that it was time for him to burgle her Reg Grundies. She figured he was a good enough bloke and she wasn't going to do much better.

He had his house, a boat, a nice car and a steady job. What more could a girl want? Plus he loved her. Maybe somewhere down the track they could do something about his wonky mince pies.

Morton was beside himself with excitement when she told him the news. 'Just you and me at the Twelve Mile Reef on Sunday,' she said. 'A beautiful lobster salad lunch, a couple of bottles of iced champagne and then an afternoon of lust. When we get tired of making love, we can have a fish for a while and then get stuck into it again.'

Moreton walked around all week like a half-opened pocketknife, clutching himself. When Sunday arrived, all was in readiness. The best lobsters, cooked especially at the fish markets that morning. Delicious salads and hot bread rolls to be washed down with a goodly supply of chilled French champagne from crystal goblets. They had even packed a linen tablecloth and proper cutlery.

God was kind and the sea was like a mirror and, as if arranged, there was not another boat in sight.

They moored up at the Twelve Mile and set the spread on the engine box that acted as a table. Knowing what was for dessert Moreton wolfed down lunch in two minutes and waited, trembling. And at last the moment he had been waiting for arrived and his darling Luna invited him to come and sit next to her and then make love.

And when it finally did happen, she couldn't believe her luck. A good sort he was not. But what a fabulous lover. Luna had hit the jackpot. Time and again he made the bells ring for her and each time was better than the previous.

By now Luna was hysterical with pleasure and the earth was moving every twenty seconds. When she screamed 'I love you', he jerked his head up so hard in triumph that his Moreton Bay Fig slipped loose and sailed about 20 feet through the air, landing in the water.

Luna almost fainted as she gazed into the crossed eyes of Yul Brynner, who was more interested in retrieving the Irish Jig, but she decided she didn't care what he looked like and threw her arms around his torso, besotted. And still in the motions of lovemaking, Moreton cast at his floating hairpiece with a tiny spinning reel and minnow lure, hooked it and as he retrieved it a bronze whaler shark came by and ate the lot.

What a sight! Moreton rugless in the raw fighting an angry whaler

on light line, with his beloved Luna wrapped around his middle, never intending to let go.

They weighed the fish and it was a new club record. We couldn't figure out why his Irish jig was covered in blood and teeth marks. We should have woke when he filled out the record claim form.

In the bit that asks 'bait used' . . . he put 'rug lure'.

Crocodile Boots

Some fisherfolk in the fish-prolific Northern Territory are totally up themselves and consider their southern cousins to be a bunch of dickheads who wouldn't know the difference between a mackerel tuna and a piano tuner. They look down their noses at southerners and tell stories in bars of their stupidity. This is one of those stories. Its origin is unknown and its truthfulness I leave to your imagination.

Fishing is full of dopes, but Merv 'Crayfish' Gibbons took the cake. He was a real dubbo. Correct height for weight he should have been about ten foot six. His girth was attributed to his constant beer swilling and the seemingly insatiable desire for hamburgers, fish and chips and deep-fried chicken.

Originally from the bush, Crayfish started off fishing the rivers and creeks around Gippsland in Victoria but moved to Sydney to chase a bit of tail around Kings Cross. He must've found a bit that didn't have wool around it 'cos he stayed — much to the ongoing torment of the poor bastards at the local fishing club that Crayfish called home.

It was a revolting sight sitting there at the Jack 'Tight Lines' McKenzie Memorial Bar, swilling piss and belching, drooling and farting over anyone silly enough to put up with his vile breath.

He thought they called him 'Crayfish' because he loved bottom fishing. You know, around the reefy cave areas, the same places where crayfish hang out. Truth is, it was because he was all arms and legs and had a head full of shit. It suited him down to the ground.

One day Crayfish announced he was taking a holiday in Darwin. The club members breathed a sigh of relief. At last a bit of peace, even if it was only for a couple of weeks.

Crayfish had teamed up with the other club idiot, Alf 'Rust' Timms, and between them they had saved enough to bunk at a cheap Darwin hotel, do a bit of fishing and stay drunk the whole time.

They shopped around and got a beaut deal at about half the normal price. Actually, the club members thought the pair had actually done something smart until they found out that they had booked in January — right in the middle of the wet season. But nobody bothered to tell them for fear they would change their minds and not go.

The story goes that they arrived in the middle of a decent blow and spent the first week lashed to the bar of the pub. As the winds subsided they decided to do a bit of shopping.

Rust (they called him that because once he was in your boat it was impossible to get him out) walked ahead while Crayfish dawdled along looking in the shop windows.

'Hey, Rust,' Crayfish yelled. 'Come and have a look at these.'

There in the bootshop, at the end of the aisle and with a dozen spotlights on them, was the most magnificent pair of boots Crayfish had ever seen in his life.

He was mesmerised. The heels were turned in, the sides buckled and the toes capped with shining gold metal, But it was the leather which captivated Bonehead.

'Fuck me, Rust. I've never seen anything like that before in my life. What are they?'

'They're crocodile boots, mate,' informed Rust.

Crayfish had to have them. ''Ow much are them boots, mate?' he asked the store attendant.

The salesman looked him up and down, noted the thongs, huge beer gut and the 'Life. Be In It' T-shirt, and came back with an accurate assessment of the situation.

'I think they're a little out of your depth, sir. About $1100 and they're yours.'

Crayfish's heart sank. Rust grabbed him by the sleeve and dragged him outside.

'You liked them, didn't you?' asked Rust.

'Sure did,' came the whimpering reply.

'Well, you can't afford to buy 'em, so why don't you get your own?' said Rust. Crayfish was confused.

'Wadda ya mean?'

'Do you realise where we are?' said Rust.

'Of course I do,' replied Crayfish, logic working overtime. 'We're in Darwin.'

'And do you know what Darwin's famous for? Let me tell you — crocodiles! There's millions of the fuckin' things. They even swim down from Borneo just to get to this prick of a place. And they eat the tourists. Fuckin' pests they are. Next thing they'll be crawlin' down the main street, nickin' kids out of their prams. The bastards are everywhere. Let's get our own crocodile boots.'

Crayfish was still confused 'How?' he asked.

'Simple,' said his mate. 'We'll rent two boats and go in different directions on one of the main creeks. That way we'll be sure to find a croc.'

And so off they went. Rust chose the northern channel and as much as he searched he couldn't find a croc anywhere.

Back at the boat-hire place, he waited in vain for Crayfish.

'You'd better go and have a look for your mate,' the boat-hire man suggested. 'He's an hour overdue and he struck me as being such a fucking dill that anything could have happened to him.'

Rust headed down the south channel, and as he rounded the first corner he nearly ran over a 16-foot crocodile, lying on its back, gasping its final breath.

Close inspection revealed its neck had been broken.

'My God,' he thought. 'Poor Crayfish . . . I hope he's okay.'

Further down the creek he rounded another bend and came across an even bigger croc — as dead as a doornail. Not only was its neck broken, but all its legs were fractured and its huge tail was bent at a right angle.

Rust was by now hysterical with worry. He sped down the creek calling for his mate. As he rounded a long bend he came across the most bizarre sight.

There was Crayfish with an Indian death-lock on a 20-footer! The

reptile's jaws were snapping and snarling and froth was spurting from its nostrils.

Rust couldn't believe his eyes. Crayfish spotted him out of the corner of his eye. 'G'day mate,' he yelled.

'Are you all right?' called Rust.

'Yeah, for the moment.'

'Need a hand?'

'No, not right now,' puffed Crayfish. 'But I'll tell ya somethin'. If this bastard hasn't got any fuckin' boots on, I'm goin' back to the pub for a beer!'

A Tall Tale of Tagged Trout

This tale was told to me many years ago by an old-timer down Swan Hill way. He wouldn't reveal his source or the origin of the story but he believed it to be true. However, after many inquiries, I couldn't find anyone who had any knowledge of a four-day Fish Festival in the district, either still running or in the past, with tagged trout. Could such an old fella have made up such an elaborate plot?

The annual four-day Fish Festival was shaping up to be a beauty. The big cash prizes on offer were attracting anglers from all over the country, and even though there were some notorious cheats among them, the organisers didn't seem to care.

With 5000 anglers at $10 a pop, they stood to make a killing, so a little fudging here and there wouldn't hurt. In fact, the rules almost encouraged it. The boundaries were anywhere within 30 kilometres of the starting point, and they weren't policed. The area included four dams and several rivers.

The big prizes were for the capture of *Terry, The Tagged Trout.* There were four Terrys — one for each dam. They were trout of about two kilograms from the local trout farm, and had been branded with an identifying tag stapled to the tail.

Amid much fuss and press coverage each year, the Terrys were released into their new homes the day before the event.

The release spots were kept secret so as not to give anyone an advantage. The four Terrys were worth $50 000 each and even the village idiot could tell you that the organisers were in deep trouble if they were all captured. In fact, even if only one were taken, it would prove embarrassing. There were also prizes of $10 000 each for the biggest Murray cod and the biggest yellowbelly. You did not need a university degree in mathematics to work out that the difference between the prize money on offer and the entry fees collected was minus $170 000 — and that was without running costs. There had to be some skulduggery afoot.

In the five years that the Fish Fest had been held, no one had ever caught a tagged fish, and the organisers had walked away with a bundle. To ensure that no one came up with the goods, the Terrys were all orally fed a slow-acting poison before release. While they looked healthy enough when photographed being thrown into the dam, they were very dead in a matter of hours.

What the organisers did not count on was one of their own being more corrupt than them. He was known as 'the Moth' because he was attracted to the light. He would get blind at the fishing club or the local and stagger home. If he saw a light on, he would invite himself in for a drink and there was no getting rid of him. He was a dreadful pest drunk, but sober he was a lot of fun.

Being an official assistant organiser and Terry-releaser, the Moth had been entrusted with the secrets of the villainy that went on. For his silence, he picked up a small share of the returns. But the Moth had got into big trouble on the punt and, with the heavies breathing down his neck for the money, he decided to out-cheat the cheats.

The only bloke he could trust with his life was an old mate of his in Sydney called Bill 'The Dago' Oliver. They called him Dago because he never stopped whingeing about the fact that his missus spent her entire life in front of the TV watching the soapies. It had been going on for years and his constant grizzle was: 'There's not a day goes by without her watching that crap.

'There's not a day goes by when she does anythin' around the house. Do ya think a bloke can get fed? No way. Fair dinkum, there's not a day goes by . . . '

Rocket scientists they were not. But between them, Dago and the Moth devised a scheme that would scoop the pool . . .

The rules of the tournament were loose, but a couple were hard and fast. There was absolutely no berleying allowed before the event, and all fish had to be weighed by 6pm sharp. Apart from that, it was open slather.

WINNER
TERRY THE TROUT
WINNER
BIGGEST COD & YELLO

COP
ELLY
WINNER
SPECIAL CATEGORY

'We'll wrap up the cod and yellowbelly sections,' the Moth had told Dago on the phone. 'I know an old cod hole about 50 kilometres out of town. When you arrive a day before the comp, I'll have 'em boilin' on the surface. Oh! And don't forget to bring your snorkel. You'll need that to catch Terry.'

A few weeks before the fish festival the Moth drove out to the cod hole that was on a big corner in a bend in the river and hung six sheep heads from the branch of an overhanging tree. He made sure to keep them hidden well within the leaves.

He returned a week later to find his self-berleying device working a treat. The sheep's heads were well and truly flyblown and the maggots were dropping into the water at a nice steady pace.

A week later every fish within 100 kilometres was waiting underneath with its head sticking out of the water and mouth open. He knew that the smaller fish such as redfin and silver perch would attract the bigger cod and yellowbellies which would eat them all and then Dago could catch them at his leisure on the first day of the comp.

Snookering Terry the Tagged Trout wasn't so simple. It wasn't until four days before the comp that the Moth and Dago devised a plan. And even then it was by a stroke of luck.

To add some authenticity to their shonky contest, the organisers announced that, due to being hounded by cheating anglers with binoculars, they would now release the four Terrys secretly, without any press watching. The media spewed. 'How do we know that you will release any fish at all?' they barked.

Amid cries of deception and fraud, the organisers agreed to let the media photograph the four boats leaving with the Terrys on board and also arranged for a trusted observer to go out with each fish-releaser.

The observers were selected from the town's most prominent and honest citizens — the police chief, the headmistress, the head of the chamber of commerce and the mayor. The Moth couldn't believe his luck. He drew his old mate the mayor, Alderman Clarrie 'Carbuncle' Carr.

Clarrie was as bald as Kojak and they called him 'Carbuncle' because he was shiny on the top and full of crap.

Carbuncle loved nothing more than a bottle of Scotch and a friendly ear. The Moth had such an ear. It would be no trouble to get Carbuncle well and truly under the weather and carry out his deception.

At the releasing of the Terrys on the eve of the comp, the flashbulbs popped as Carbuncle and the Moth held Terry up in his plastic bag for all to see. 'Take your time,' the organisers had told the Moth. 'Don't make it obvious where you're heading to let the trout go. And don't let Carbuncle see you give it the poison. Otherwise we'll be paying him blackmail forever.'

The Moth putt-putted a couple of kilometres around the lake before he pulled in at Knot's Pier for the couple of bottles of Scotch he had hidden there the previous day. He primed Carbuncle with one and it wasn't long before the mayor was dribbling and talking about all the slings he'd taken over the years.

The Moth then loaded a block of concrete with a wire handle on board, explaining to his drunken friend that it was ballast in case a breeze came up. And off they went.

They went straight to Mackenzie's Flats — the shallowest part of the dam, where no one had caught a fish in years. Here the Moth tied a hundred metres of sash cord to the concrete block and lowered it over the side. When it hit the bottom a few metres down, he removed Terry from his bag, tied the other end of the sash cord through its gills, stuffed the poison capsule up its rear end and threw it overboard for Dago to find in the morning.

Carbuncle was oblivious to all this because he was out cold on the bottom of the boat. The Moth got stuck into the other bottle of Scotch and, by the time Carbuncle woke from his drunken stupor, the Moth was skiting about the exact location of the maggot-berleyed cod hole, the tethered trout and how clever he and Dago were.

The cunning old mayor, now sober, listened intently.

When the cops hauled the Moth in the following day and questioned him about the body they had found — the person had apparently drowned when he got tangled up in a length of sash cord at Mackenzie's Flats — he denied any knowledge of it.

Apparently the victim, complete with snorkel, had been diving toward the bottom and had become entangled in the cord because whoever had tied the fish to the end of it had jammed something up its backside causing it to blow up with air and float to the top.

'That explains why they told me ten times to shove the poison capsule down its gob,' the Moth thought to himself as he examined the trout the police had found attached to the sash cord.

'But that's funny,' he thought. 'Where's the tag?' The Moth was puzzled and upset. His partner in crime was dead and the tag was missing. What was going on? asked the police. Had they seen anything that night? After all they had headed out in that direction.

'No, sir,' the Moth replied and Carbuncle backed him up.

The cops didn't connect the Moth with the late Dago Oliver and Carbuncle wasn't saying anything. By a strange coincidence, the brother of the guy who found Dago's body, who by an even stranger coincidence happened to be Carbuncle's nephew, turned in a Terry that very afternoon and claimed the fifty grand.

As the tag was only just stuck to the tail and not stapled on, and the trout was only about one kilo instead of two kilos, the organisers smelt a giant rat, but they couldn't do a thing about it. They had to fork out the money.

And by an even more extraordinary coincidence, Carbuncle's son weighed in a huge cod and a yellowbelly that same day and picked up a cool twenty grand. No one could figure out why maggots kept dropping out of their gobs at the weigh-in. The organisers were out of pocket, the cops had an unexplained corpse, Carbuncle came into a lot of money all of a sudden, and the Moth left town.

They say he's been sighted around Bondi, where the lights are on 24 hours a day.

The Sharks of Sugartown

This supposedly true story is Sugartown folklore and was told to me by the locals when I was forced to stay there overnight when my friend's Porsche blew a radiator hose. Sugartown doesn't have a Porsche dealership.

Broadwater is on the Pacific Highway between Ballina and Grafton on the north coast of New South Wales. Because the local industry is sugar, the tiny township is better known as 'Sugartown'.

Consisting of a pub, a service station and the usual small collection of country shops, the highlight of Sugartown is the NRMA depot, on the highway opposite the pub. From their regular possies at the bar, the locals watch the procession of vehicles and occupants towed into the depot daily. Most of these poor wretches have broken down along the highway. A call for help by a friendly farmer has them under tow in no time at all to the comforts of the depot, where the measure of their dilemma is assessed and the appropriate action taken.

In most cases the vehicles can be repaired on the spot, but when special parts are needed, a stay in the rooms at the back of the Exchange Hotel can be arranged until the bits are flown up from Sydney. This usually takes a day and a night.

Such is the case of the American tourist, Charlie 'just call me Chuck' Schuster, in his rented Cadillac. The poor bastard had blown a fanbelt about 20 kilometres out of town and was rescued by none other than 'Knowledge', the local know-all and urger who just happened to be passing by in his shitbox ute.

On the drive into town they became great mates. Chuck was overwhelmed by his rescuer's assistance. Back at the NRMA depot, Knowledge arranged for the Caddie to be towed to town, and when it

©BEB97

was discovered that it had blown an alternator and the parts wouldn't arrive until the day after tomorrow, he arranged accommodation at the Exchange and an introduction to everyone who was anyone in the bar at the pub.

Knowledge had told Chuck that it was just 'good old Aussie hospitality'. Of course the tourist had no way of knowing that somewhere along the line it was going to have a dramatic effect on his wallet . . . Knowledge hadn't figured out the angle yet, but it was only a matter of time.

The following morning Chuck expressed his enthusiasm for fishing to his new best friend.

'Say, buddy', he said, pointing to the Richmond River in the background. 'Do you guys ever catch any fish in that creek?'

'That creek, as you call it,' laughed Knowledge, 'just happens to produce the best shark fishing in the district — probably in Australia, for that matter.'

'You're bullshittin' me!' said the Yank in amazement. 'Surely no self-respecting shark would live there. It looks like it's runnin' upside down!'

Now Knowledge made it up as he went. There was a quid to be made here somewhere.

'No, not there,' Knowledge said, 'much further downriver, towards the sea. A mate of mine's got a private island that's only accessible by boat. He catches white pointers, tigers, makos — you name it, the joints crawlin' with 'em. They gather there in their thousands to feed on the run of giant sea mullet that gather at the mouth of the river to spawn about this time every year.'

'Trouble is, the spot's very exclusive and no one knows about it,' he continued. 'There's even a secret path through the canefields to get to the beach and a boat to row out there. Just don't fall in on the way out. I can get ya out there if you really wanna go for the day. But I'd say for sure that it's gunna cost ya.'

'How much?' Chuck asked.

'I'm not really sure,' Knowledge replied, putting his toe in the water to see how warm it was. 'I reckon that mates' rates would be about a hundred bucks a day — that's the use of the boat and the whole island. Reckon I can get him down to eighty for you, seein' as you're a tourist and all. Wadda ya reckon about that?'

'That's a deal mate,' Chuck said and put out his hand and shook on it. 'I'll get my gear out of the Caddie and we'll start right away.'

The 'gear' turned out to be a beach rod and one of those cheap Japanese spinning reels. The Yank had bought it for catching whiting at Port Stephens, on the way through to Sydney.

'About as useful as a club foot in a bushfire,' said Knowledge, observing the gear. 'They'll smash that kid's stuff to rat shit. What you need is some heavy shark gear, about 50 kilo breaking-strain line, a game-fishing reel and a good stout rod. Mate of mine's got just the outfit and he rents it out to guys lucky enough to get out to the island. I'll see how much he'll charge me for the day. I reckon about twenty bucks should cover it.'

'OK, let's go,' the Yank said, keen to get among the sharks.

'Hold it,' said Knowledge. 'What about traces and hooks? You're going to look pretty stupid out there with elephant gun gear and yellowtail hooks. I'll slip down to the hardware store and get it while you get changed. Give us twenty bucks, that should be enough. No it won't, you'll also need bait, say half-a-dozen mullet, so you'd better make that an even fifty.'

The Yank handed Knowledge the money. 'Tell you what I'll do,' Knowledge said. 'I'll even run you up there and back — and the petrol's on me.'

It took Knowledge about ten minutes to 'borrow' Bluey Howard's shark rod, reel and traces from his open garage. He wouldn't miss it for a day; he only used it when he went big-game fishing down the coast.

Another ten minutes to knock off six poddy mullet from Oodles Bourke's mullet trap in the river behind the stock and station agent's and he was back at the Exchange, looking for his punter.

Chuck was waiting, resplendent in sandals, long black socks, knee-length shorts, yellow and lime-green open-neck shirt, sunglasses, Panama hat and a cigar that was as long and as round and the same colour as a respectable sized dog's turd.

'These Aussies are real friendly to tourists,' Chuck thought to himself as they sped toward the 'secret spot', about two kilometres out of town.

The 'secret path' was about 10 metres wide and led straight through the Turner brothers' cane fields. In fact it wasn't a path at all, it was a divider between the sugarcane crops, and it led down to a sandy little beach where the brothers kept their small dinghy — they occasionally fished the river for bream.

Without the divider, access to the beach was impossible as the crops grew right to the water's edge. The brothers didn't mind if anyone used it to get to the beach, as long as they asked permission first. Knowledge was not the type to bother with such trivialities.

'Watch out for the snakes in the sugarcane,' Knowledge warned his new chum. 'The joint's crawlin' with 'em, all sorts of the bastards — death adders, copperheads, red-bellied black snakes — and all deadly poisonous. They live in the cane fields and only come out when they burn it, but if you walk on one on the edge of the cane field, you'll get bit for sure.'

The Yank fled the length of the open space in double-quick time. Knowledge tried to keep up with him but found it hard as he was laughing so much. He knew full well the snakes stayed in the cane unless something drove them out.

The exclusive island was about 100 metres out into the river. Knowledge showed Chuck how to use the oars, loaded his gear and pushed him off.

'See you back here at five,' he yelled. The Yank waved as Knowledge headed toward the pub for an icy cold ale and to hold court about the nice mug he had in tow. He counted his money on the way — a hundred and thirty dollars, not bad for a morning's work! Wait till the fellas hear this one!

By 2pm, Knowledge was well and truly flyblown. He decided to wander into the TAB and have a punt. An omen presented itself immediately. 'Give me fifty bucks on *Yankee Tourist* in the third,' he yelled, throwing his money down.

Of course *Yankee Tourist* bolted in at 20 to 1. Knowledge couldn't

believe his luck — what a day! More drinks all round back at the Exchange and it was time to go. Lugging a carton of cans, Knowledge headed back to the beach to wait for his sucker to arrive back sharkless — he would explain that there had been a sudden turn in the tide or make up some other bullshit to pacify him. Besides, he had the Yank's money . . . so who cared.

As drunk as he was, Knowledge could still make out the boat on the island but he could see no Yank. He tried to ponder the significance of this but passed out in the warm sand.

Chuck soon figured out there was something peculiar about shark fishing prospects on 'the island', as the water around it for about 20 metres out was very shallow and sandy and after an hour of patient angling his cunningly-rigged mullet was still untouched.

He decided to take a walk around to the other side of the island. A few minutes later he parted some bushes to find, to his absolute astonishment, a bridge linking the island to the mainland, and several people on the bridge pulling in bream, flathead and whiting galore . . . he had tumbled onto the local hot spot.

The penny still hadn't dropped as he inquired of an angler fishing from the bridge, 'Caught any sharks?'

The angler laughed. 'Are you crazy, mister? The last shark seen around here was when the local car dealer fell in!'

Many thoughts crossed the Yank's mind as he walked back toward the boat and shark alley.

The first sign of trouble was when Knowledge felt the hot ashes falling all over him. He ignored them at first, brushing the cinders from his hair and face and nuzzling back into the beer carton, now his makeshift pillow.

More hot ashes then roaring and heat. 'Shit no, a cane-field fire,' Knowledge screamed, as he realised that he was about to wind up medium rare.

The Turner brothers had chosen today to put the fire through their cane fields (they did this once every season) and now it was heading toward the river, the way it always did, fanned along by a late-afternoon sou'wester.

Knowledge woke to a towering wall of smoke and fire heading in his direction at a rapid rate of knots.

But that was the least of his worries. He nearly died of shock when he saw what was wriggling out of it. Snakes! Hundreds of them, in all shapes and sizes. And all of 'em were heading for his little beach.

There were two alternatives: be bitten or drown. Knowledge had never bothered to learn to swim. Neither option seemed a good choice.

Then a third possibility presented itself. Sitting out in mid-channel was Chuck, in his little boat, totally in awe of the spectacle as the flames roared hundreds of feet in the air and the sugarcane fire roared deafeningly.

It looked as if the gates of hell had opened up, yet in a few short minutes it would be all over as the fire reached the river bank, the end of its journey and most certainly the end of Knowledge, either from the flames or a deadly snakebite.

A huge fat death adder hissed and jabbed its forked tongue at Knowledge as he hit it between the eyes with a beer can.

'Give us a hand, will ya mate!' he screamed and frantically waved to Chuck.

'Why don't you jump in and swim out to the boat, buddy,' Chuck called back, obviously enjoying his opportunity to even up. 'Or are you scared of the sharks? You needn't be, 'cos there aren't any.'

The beach was now a wriggling mass of serpents.

'Please mate, ya gotta help me,' Knowledge shrieked.

'All right,' said the Yank, 'But it'll cost ya.'

'How much?'

'How much have you got?' asked the Yank.

'I got a grand,' said Knowledge, wading knee-deep in death adders as he produced his winnings and held them up for the Yank to see.

'Well, the going rate for a rescue of this sort ought to be a couple of grand, but seeing as you're a local and all . . . '

And the Yank was laughing his head off as he picked up the oars.

The Duck, the Chemist and Billy the Pig

Some fish fight better than others, and everyone who dangles a line has their own preference. But some species are just so darn ornery that tales of their capture, or at least the attempts at their capture, are fishing folklore around the world. Here are a couple of the best.

Ask any of the boys at the fishing club what's the best fighting fish in the world, and if there are 10 blokes there, they'll give you 10 different answers. There's certainly no outright winner.

Legendary American fishing and western writer Zane Grey was always in awe of the broadbill swordfish — the 'broadsworded gladiator', as he called it. He caught many in his long and illustrious career, but one story will always stick out in my mind.

Fishing at Santa Catalina off California, Grey elected to put his brother, Red, onto a broadbill. They hooked a fish of good size and the battle raged for three hours until Red could fight the fish no more.

Grey's boatman, the legendary Captain Laurie Mitchell, was ushered to the fighting chair. Mitchell was no slouch on the rod, as he was then the world black marlin record-holder.

Although they were aware that a second angler taking the rod disqualified the fish from any record claim, they still fought on for the sheer sport of having such a mighty fighting fish on the end of the line.

After four hours in the fighting chair, Mitchell had to concede defeat. The huge fish had beaten him to a standstill. In the gathering dusk Zane Grey, considered at the time to be the greatest angler in the world, took the chair and lay into the greenheart rod with fresh vigour.

EXT
SURGERY
&
ITCHEN

The battle raged on into the night. For another two hours the master angler pumped and wound, gaining line at every opportunity and giving it back equally as the fish showed no signs of giving in.

Then the strangest thing happened. Although they couldn't see far into the dead calm distance, they could hear splashing noises. Then line would peel from the reel, followed by a much larger splashing noise and then silence. Then, the same splashing noises again and another spasmodic burst of line. Grey was mystified.

Another large splash. The gallant fish was jumping from the water in short bursts. But in a bid to escape? If the fish was that tired, surely they would have boated it by now.

Then it dawned on Grey what was happening. The small splashing noises were flying fish re-entering the water after jumping and the broadbill was feeding on them.

After nine hours of constant attack on heavy gear the fish had started feeding, as though it had never been hooked. It was chasing and pouncing on the flying fish — as fresh as the moment the battle started.

In disbelief, and probably out of respect, Grey cut the line and headed for home in the dark.

Having never caught a broadbill, or for that matter ever even hooked one, I must choose my toughest fighters from less exotic species, and to my mind, yellowfin tuna, giant trevally, whaler sharks with their long pectoral fins, bonefish and kingfish all rate among the top fighters.

But if you asked a long time ago mate of mine, Peter 'The Duck' King, what he regarded as the toughest fish in the ocean was, he would have told you every time . . . black drummer. Or pigs, as they're more commonly known because of their dirty fighting habits.

Like kingfish and southern Australian blue groper, pigs are filthy fighters. They delight in grabbing a bait and heading straight back into their cave with it. And if it just so happens to have your hook in it . . . then it's an instant bust-up. Goodnight Dick.

But pigs don't do this because they know that there's a very sharp hook inside the morsel they have just mouthed. Oh no! And they haven't figured out that if they run your line over the rocks a barnacles at the entrance to their cave, they will bust you off.

No way. That's the stuff rocket scientists are made of and a drummer, or any fish for that matter, could hardly be classified as a candidate for MENSA. Besides, if they were that smart, they wouldn't take your bait in the first place.

No, they duck out of their cave or apartment beneath a ledge, grab what's on offer and duck back in the front door as quick as they can before they get mugged by another drummer trying to take the morsel from them. And if your line happens to be attached to it . . . stiff cheddar. You're busted.

It's as simple as that. Believe me, there are no table manners in Fishville.

So, obviously, the best tactics with an ambush fighter like the pig is to sink the hook quickly and hang on for grim death, hoping to turn the fish's head and at least get it coming your way before it can get back inside its front door.

And these same tactics apply to other notorious ambush feeders, such as the legendary New Guinea black bass. And the giant kingfish that have taken up permanent and extremely territorial residence in the caves honeycombed along the rock ledges of Jervis Bay in southern New South Wales.

The Duck, an extremely tough ex-front row rugby union player and an equally extremely tough plain-clothes detective, thought that we called him by his nickname because his abbreviated name was P. King, as in Peking duck, the tasty Chinese dish.

He was such a tough bastard that we let him go on thinking that.

But it was really because he spoke with a savage speech impediment where he replaced his 'r's' with 'w's'. And what with being a copper and a savage rooter at the same time, he was always either trying to crack onto a sheila or crack a case that he was working on.

'See that sheila over there. I'm gunna cwack onto her tonight,' he would say, his speech impediment working overtime.

Or, 'We're about to cwack that big jewellewy wobbewy in West Wyde.'

Or, 'I'll never forget the time we cwacked Wandwick's defence and I scored on the wight wing.'

Cwack, cwack. That's really why we called him The Duck. But no one was letting on.

The Duck had been fishing this one secret spot at North Bondi for years, with great success on a bit better than average sized pigs around three to five kilograms. But they came at a price.

All this time he had been having a running battle with one giant resident pig. It had grown to enormous proportions, thanks to The Duck's continued berleying over the years with loaves of bread in an effort to entice and catch its mates.

The big pig and The Duck saw so much of each other that The Duck even had a name for his antagonist. He named it Billy, after the famous hotel in Bondi Junction, *Billy The Pig's*.

He had hooked that big old pig at least a dozen times, and each time, Billy had smashed him up. Billy had caused The Duck enough headaches and he had to go.

So The Duck devised a plan. A two-man plan. And the other party had to be able to keep a secret, because The Duck didn't want anyone else to know his secret spot.

Such a person was The All-night Chemist, so named because he never shut up. The Chemist was a fanatical beach fisherman, and while he could talk underwater in an army overcoat with the pockets full of pennies, he was also good with a secret, providing that he was told that it was a secret and to keep his gob shut. The Chemist gave his word.

For two months prior to his planned assault on Billy the Pig, The Duck selected the juiciest and plumpest cunji and cabbage he could find, mixed it up with luscious Botany Bay weed with the weevils in it and berleyed his spot like buggery.

But he didn't fish; he just berleyed, every day at precisely the same time. After a month Billy was well and truly conned, the memories of bygone battles long forgotten, and was waiting for him.

At the end of six weeks Billy was on the surface, lying on his back in close with his gob open, waiting to be hand-fed. The Duck could almost reach out and pat it.

'Shitbwained fish,' he said to The Chemist, 'now I'm gunna dwive it nuts.' The Duck returned to his secret spot every day, but now with no berley. Billy was waiting patiently for him, and when The Duck didn't feed him, the poor demented fish almost climbed up the rocks.

The Duck had Billy exactly where he wanted him. It was time to put the plan into action.

He had built a special rod for the occasion. It consisted of a blank made out of the toughest space-age graphite in the world — it would load itself up like a pole-vaulter's pole, launching the jumper over the bar as soon as the fish grabbed the bait and headed for its cave.

The idea was that once the fish took off, the rod would allow it to go so far and then, when bent to its limit, the rod would recoil the other way so fiercely that it would either turn the fish or rip its head off.

For a reel he borrowed a huge Shimano Tiagra, loaded with 130 pound breaking-strain line that was normally used to catch giant black marlin at Cairns, and he cranked the reversible drag up to the limit, ensuring that no matter what, the fish wasn't going to get one inch of line off that reel.

The Duck had also designed a special shoulder and back harness, complete with gimballed rod bucket and reel clips that attached him permanently to the rod and reel.

The Chemist's job was to stand behind The Duck, firmly hanging onto a length of rope that was attached to the harness and making sure that The Duck wouldn't get dragged into the drink by the power of Billy The Pig in full retreat.

With all in readiness The Duck fed Billy the biggest, juiciest piece of cunji imaginable, and when the big fish took off with it he leaned back into the rod and set the hook. The reaction was instant. Billy sensed that something was dramatically wrong, and headed flat out for his cave, stretching the line to its limit and bending the rod almost to breaking point.

What happened next will never be known, but the general opinion is that Billy had a heart attack and died on the spot. And with suddenly no resistance from the fish, The Duck fell over backwards onto The

Chemist as the recoil of the rod launched the giant pig into mid-air. When it reached the end of its tether, it rocketed earthwards and embedded itself in The Duck's face, as dead as a Randwick favourite.

The Chemist cracked up.

'Get this wotten thing off me,' The Duck begged, but try as he may, The Chemist couldn't lift the fish. He soon discovered why.

'Look at this!' he exclaimed. 'The old bastard's got about twenty hooks hangin' out of him from where he's been hooked all those times and they've all embedded in your face. I can't cut 'em out and I can't pull 'em out. I'll have to take you to Emergency with the fish attached to you and they can get him off you.'

The Duck was in a bad way for a long time, with his face very badly cut up from the hooks. He ended up very badly scarred. I didn't see much of him after that, but they tell me that some nights when the coppers all get together at the *Bourbon and Beefsteak* in the Cross for a few drinks, if you look closely at the Duck's face in the right light when he's pissed, you can match the scars up, and they read 'Billy'.

Love on the Rocks

'Rockhoppers', we call 'em. That unique breed of Aussie anglers who fish the incredibly dangerous rock ledges and reefs that make up the coastline of a good part of Australia. And along the Beecroft Peninsula, on the northern side of Jervis Bay (on the south coast of New South Wales), God has erected fishing platforms that could only be considered by the rockhopper as gifts from heaven. It is as if they were designed with the fisherman in mind.

It's enough to send a dedicated rockhopper troppo. Long rock ledges that plummet 30 metres directly to the ocean's floor at the angler's feet. The many caves that honeycomb these submerged cliff faces are home to huge kingfish, and the swirling blue-water currents that come from the north during the summer months and bounce off these undersea mountains bring with them species you would only expect to catch on a boat.

Most of the tunas — yellowfin, striped, mackerel, northern and southern bluefin, bonito and frigate mackerel — as well as salmon, tailor, trevally, wahoo, Spanish mackerel and the occasional sailfish and marlin have all been caught here. Off the rocks!

Mindboggling? It certainly is. It's little wonder then that this area is recognised as the greatest rockfishing paradise in the world. And there's no shortage of bottom species: snapper, huge bream, blackfish, morwong, barracouta, groper and drummer, to name but a few.

Rockfishing wouldn't be the sport it is today if it wasn't for places like the Devil's Gorge, Little and Big Beecroft, The Drum and Drumsticks and Crocodile Head. It was at these piscatorial paradises that the original high-speed spinning reel, the Australian-made Seascape, the incredibly successful WK Arrow lures and the four-metre fibreglass rods were initially used against fish that just weren't meant to be caught off the rocks on such primitive tackle.

The poor old Seascape's gears used to strip, the spools would buckle and the handles bend, but somehow or other we caught the fish, even if it meant carrying six Seascapes each. Besides, they were the only reel available in the late '60s and early '70s with 6 to 1 retrieve, quick enough to ship the lure across the surface so that it resembled a scurrying garfish, driving the tuna nuts and inducing them to strike at it.

Any new product could be given a true test at places like The Gorge because, like all the other spots along the peninsula, it was guaranteed to produce fish. The hammering we gave those Seascapes paved the way for the sophisticated, modern-day Shimano and Daiwa high-speed retrieve reels with their 6 to 1 ratios.

I keep saying 'we' because I was there in the beginning, the late '60s and early '70s, with guys like Tom Nairne, Lyn Donohue, Kevin Lemon and Jack Erskine, all legends in rockfishing circles.

The catches were extraordinary by anyone's standards. In one season Lyn and I caught over a ton of tuna each from the rocks. We hooked a marlin and got smashed up a hundred times by huge kingies that cruised out of their caves to mug a bonito or frigate mackerel which we had fought to the rock face.

And all of this was on lures, no live baits. We were what they called 'purists'. We refused to use anything but lures, maintaining that if a big fish is caught on a live bait, then its fighting qualities can be severely restricted if the bait is swallowed deep and the hook penetrates a vital organ or nerve. With lures, they can only be hooked in the mouth, and the fight is not inhibited.

As a boy, I had lain awake at night reading the fascinating tales of the spinmen along the classic deep-water ledges at the southernmost tip of South Africa.

With rangoon and split-cane rods and Penn 49 reels, they caught huge bluefin tuna, some of them over 100 pounds, off the rocks on lures throughout the '50s and '60s.

The old Forty-Niners were really an overhead game-fishing reel

with an unusually large spool. The spool's diameter was so large that one complete turn of the handle would retrieve as much line as a normal-sized reel with 6 to 1 ratio.

Somehow they managed to cast up to 150 yards with those big old clunkers, and then they wound like buggery, retrieving the white 6 ounce painted lead lures quickly enough to con the bluefin into thinking they were wounded bait fish scurrying away, and therefore easy pickings. Mind you, our South African friends were no sports fishermen.

Unlike us with our 8–10 kilogram line, they used 15–30 kilogram breaking-strain line, and the minute one of those finned missiles hooked up, they cranked up the drag on the reel and hung on for dear life. If they could get its head around and get a direct pull on it, they had a better-than-even chance of catching it. If it swam away, gathering momentum as it went, then there was no hope, unless the fish made a mistake.

I promised myself that if I ever got the chance to catch huge fish off the rocks, it would be on lures, to maximise the fight. The Devil's Gorge gave me that opportunity. But specialising in lure fishing exclusively had its drawbacks.

It seemed the really big fish weren't interested in artificial enticements, and while we took yellowfin and northern bluefin tuna of up to 20 kilograms on lures, the whopper yellowfin of around 50 kilograms, and the occasional marlin, would follow the lure briefly and then, with a flick of the tail, disappear.

Lyn hooked a small marlin one day, but in the twinkling of an eye it jumped off. Deep down, we both knew we'd never get into the history books for catching the first yellowfin over 45 kilograms, or the first marlin anywhere in the world, from the rocks. That would have to be on a live bait.

Sure enough, in 1970 Tom Nairne caught a 47 kilogram yellowfin off the rocks at the Devil's Gorge on a live trevally. The fact that it was taken on a four-metre rod that was as sloppy as a piece of licorice, a Policansky reel, and only 14 kilogram breaking-strain line, made the catch even more astonishing. Tom had created history.

Then, in the summer of 1971, an unidentified angler cracked the jackpot. A 30 kilogram black marlin was taken from the rocks at Beecroft, a couple of miles north of Devil's Gorge. At first it was too astonishing to believe. The world's most sought-after game fish, the one that anglers in those antiquated times would go for years without catching in boats, had been caught off the rocks!

But it was true. And you guessed it, it was taken on a live bait. That catch opened the floodgates and made the Beecroft Peninsula the mecca for land-based game fishing.

Since then, there have been dozens of marlin caught off the rocks, most of them coming from a spot called the Torpedo Tubes, which is actually inside Jervis Bay. But as astonished as we were then, improved technology and techniques have ensured that modern-day captures make Tom's 47 kilogram yellowfin and that first-ever 30 kilogram marlin from the rocks look like tiddlers.

A couple of years back, Vic Caplicas landed a 100 kilogram (that's 222 pounds!!!) black marlin off the rocks at Beecroft Peninsula, but only after a two-hour battle which saw the huge fish peel off 800 metres of line in one burst and nearly empty the reel. And if that hasn't knocked you out of your seat, then cop this. It was caught on a 10 kilogram breaking-strain line. That fish was twelve times heavier than the line it was caught on. Again, it was a live bait.

And if any of you out there have ever caught a yellowfin tuna, you'll know that they are the toughest thing that swims, one of the most sought-after game fish in the world. A 50 kilogram fish is a bottler. A 60 kilogram yellowfin is a heartstopper. Anything over that is 'I've died and gone to heaven' material. Out of a boat, that is, where you can follow the fish until it tires.

Off the rocks, a 50 kilogram fish is unbelievable. They're like an express train, and impossible to stop. Then how the hell did Theo Papaulias catch a 75 kilogram (that's 155 pounds) yellowfin off the stones at the Beecroft Peninsula a few years ago? Admittedly, it was on a 25 kilogram line, but even out of a boat that's backbreaking work, because there's just no stopping them.

'There's no real secret to it,' Theo told me. 'Just keep trying. I lost a few before I caught that one and while you need lots of luck, it's a case of hanging on and never giving up. Twice that fish had me down to only a couple of yards of line on the reel and each time I turned him. Oh! Just one other thing. I was using live bait,' he winked.

And since Theo's extraordinary catch, 22-year-old Ben MacLean landed a 92 kilogram yellowfin from the rocks at Green Cape in southern New South Wales, becoming the first angler to top the old 200 pound mark for a yellowfin from the rocks since John Derkacz set the benchmark back in April 1978.

Staggering catches? You betcha. To my mind, the guys who fish for and catch these mighty warriors of the deep from a land-based position are the greatest anglers of them all. I salute all of them.

Things that Float

You never know what you'll find floating around out there in the middle of the ocean, and running into solid objects in a boat causes more disaster than most other boating hazards combined. But apart from being a danger, floating objects are also fish havens, so it's always worth a look to see what's living underneath them.

Every time I read that a boat at sea has gone missing without a trace, I automatically wonder what it hit. There are so many floating objects out there that going to sea these days is like tap-dancing through a minefield.

I've seen humpback, pilot and southern right whales, countless sunfish, shipping containers, huge tree trunks, dead dogs, sheep and cattle, and even an old Silent Knight refrigerator floating around in the ocean.

Every one of them is capable of sinking your boat and killing you if you hit it.

Any ocean-going fisho will tell you that floating debris (the bigger the better) is a godsend, because huge concentrations of fish, usually mahi-mahi and kingfish, congregate under it and are easy to catch. But more of that later.

Floating objects are much more treacherous than they are useful as fish attractors.

Boats decked out with the latest in safety equipment have disappeared off the face of the earth without so much as a bleep from an EPIRB or a mayday over the radio. When you consider that it takes only seconds to activate the radio beacon or get on the two-way, those boats must have gone down pretty darn quickly.

There's no doubt that the most treacherous things that float are the huge containers which fall off the container ships and float about 45 centimetres below the surface. If you hit one, it's goodnight Dick — they open up the front of the boat like a can of sardines, and it sinks instantly.

I imagine it happens so quickly that you're drowning before you know what's happened. No doubt there are people in the world who've hit containers and survived, but I've yet to meet one.

I heard a whisper that there were moves afoot to produce a device that would sink containers after they'd been in the water for a specified time. Something like a dissolvable bung which would eventually let water in so the container could sink to the bottom.

A fantastic idea, but would the container companies outlay an arm and a leg to sink a fortune's worth of whatever and lose all hope that one day it might be recovered and returned by another ship?

Besides, the needle-in-the-haystack odds that a vessel would run into one tell us that you would have more chance of being trampled by a multi-tufted, three-legged Bavarian wildebeest while flying on the Concorde from Fiji to Tasmania with Frank Sinatra driving and Madonna pouring the drinks naked.

Most boats that come to grief in the shipping lanes of the world are either commercial fishermen or long-distance yachties. Us recreational anglers rarely venture out that far, but we still have a lot to contend with in the way of floating debris, particularly after torrential rain, which flushes out the creeks and rivers into the estuaries. Anything — from dead animals to bales of hay — can be swept out to sea.

I'd like a dollar for every time we've sucked a plastic garbage bag up into the engine cooling intake of the boat or got one caught around the propeller on the outboard. But that's one of the facts of boating life. I doubt that people will ever learn that plastic bags are the worst possible thing you can throw overboard and are probably responsible for more boating mishaps than any other 10 items combined.

The beautiful old sunfish has got a lot to answer for as well. I'd hate to think how many boaties I know have bent a prop or damaged their hull by running over a sunfish as it lolled around on the surface with its giant fin flopping from side to side.

The huge, moon-shaped sunfish grow up to a ton and are as deadly as a floating mine, should you hit one. That aside, they're the most lovable creature that swims, neither carnivore nor predator, preferring to graze on bluebottle, jellyfish and plankton.

To my mind, a lot of the boats that disappear without trace within sight of land have probably been going too fast and hit a sunfish. Although they can do plenty of damage and most definitely cause death, I know of a dozen boats that have hit them and lived to tell the tale.

Floating logs are another deathtrap, and while I've only ever seen a couple of floating containers, I've seen more than my fair share of logs.

Some of the commercial logs I've seen defy the imagination, and I can only assume they must have fallen off log-carrying vessels. The biggest I have ever seen off Sydney was about 30 metres long, at least 10 metres around and trimmed of its branches. It was floating with the north-to-south current just off Sydney Heads, and underneath it were thousands of small mahi-mahi (dolphin fish) and rat kingies up to three kilograms.

Marine biologist Dr Julian Pepperell tells me that all species of fish congregate under floating objects because it's a 'reference point in an otherwise featureless void'. In other words, it's like a dunny in the desert. Dr Julian also believes that the shadows of debris and any ropes that may be attached to the log provide cover in which fish hide. Big fish eat smaller fish, and the longer the log is in the water, the more it becomes an important part of the food chain for that area.

I'd often wondered what would congregate around a floating log in an area notorious for huge fish — such as like off the Great Barrier Reef, a place where the predators have nicknames like 'the razor gang' and in turn are eaten by game fish and sharks the size of which the brain cannot comprehend.

Well, a few years ago I got to find out, and if I live to be 1000 I doubt that I will ever see the likes of it again.

Fishing for black marlin with Captain Dennis 'Brazakka' Wallace off the No. 7 Ribbon Reef, about 160 kilometres north of Cairns and

45 miles out to sea, he spotted on the horizon what he thought was a life raft with three people on it. We pulled in the baits and steamed towards it.

It turned out to be the top three to four metres of a huge log which was sitting upright in the water. Its diameter would have been the equivalent of a 10-man life raft. The water was crystal clear, but no matter how hard we gazed into it, there was just no end to that log. At a guess I would say it was 30 metres to 50 metres long.

And gathered around it was the largest congregation of big fish and sharks I have ever seen in my life. There were huge marlin, mahi-mahi, tuna, wahoo, mackerel, rainbow runners and heaps of whaler sharks. The first lure cast at the tree was engulfed the second it hit the water as the fish elbowed each other out of the way to get at it.

We would have caught a squillion fish if it hadn't been for the predators. The minute something hooked up it was eaten by something bigger: either a mackerel, wahoo or a shark. We watched in awe as a huge marlin swam among them and then disappeared into the abyss, obviously too full to bother hassling them.

After we'd had some fun, Brazakka put out a couple of big trolling lures and dragged them in a wide circle around the protruding log. The hook-up was almost instant and as the big Shimano Tiagra reel yielded the 80 pound line to what was obviously a huge fish, we put first-time angler Steve Meads in the chair.

That big black marlin jumped all over the joint and as it was Steve's first decent game fish, we took it and weighed it at 350 kilograms. We hate killing them, but it's acceptable for an angler to take his first catch and then to never kill another.

That log was just like an aquarium, the likes of which I'll probably never see again. It didn't look like a commercial log and Brazakka said it was probably thousands of years old and could have been uprooted and washed down the Amazon to somehow wind up as a fish haven in the Pacific. It's an experience that will live with me all my life.

So what is there to learn from floating objects? They kill and they provide life. Watch out for them . . . and always look for fish beneath them.

They'll Eat Anything

So you think fish are smart, and very particular about their diets? The wily old bream. The cunning flathead. Wrong. Given the right circumstances, fish will eat anything, and the less likely the morsel, the more they seem to like it.

A popular urban myth told time and again is the one about how some gangsters threw an unfaithful associate in the drink and then attracted the sharks to him by pouring buckets of bullock's blood into the water.

Not true. Yes, I know you've heard it in one form or another before and you believe it to be true, but I'm here to tell you that it's a load of bullock's, so to speak.

Why? Simple. Under normal circumstances sharks are not attracted to land-animal blood, and that's that.

Mind you, that's not to say that they couldn't become fond of it if there were an abattoir pumping blood and animal offal into the ocean on a permanent basis, but land-based animals are not really on a shark's diet — fish, whales, seals, dolphins and other sea creatures are.

But there are exceptions to every rule. Remember the dog that went missing in the water in *Jaws*? As factually absurd as *Jaws* was, that was one true bit. But among some preposterous blunders was this next little gem.

Remember the ill-fated Captain Quint (Robert Shaw) sitting in the cabin telling Richard Dreyfuss and Roy Scheider how he survived the sinking of the *USS Indianapolis* in 1945?

'We was returnin' to Pearl Harbor after deliverin' the bomb when we was torpedoed and the *Indianapolis* sank within minutes,' Quint recalled in American/Irish drawl. 'Seein' as our mission was top secret, no one knew our predicament. Eight hundred of us took to the water and after four days and five nights, when help finally arrived, only 200 of us survived. The rest were eaten by the sharks.'

Absolute crap. History books tell us that on that fateful day when the *Indianapolis* went down, almost 500 men perished in the water by drowning, dehydration or whatever, but only 60 to 80 of them were actually taken by sharks.

That, and the fact that white pointers don't stalk humans, as the critter with the IQ of a brain surgeon in all the *Jaws* movies did, are possibly the two greatest lies about sharks ever laid on a gullible public.

Yet *Jaws* was certainly one of the most frightening movies of all time, if you're prepared to overlook the glaring blunders.

But back to the plot. Yes, sharks do eat dogs. That bit is true. They eat dogs with regular monotony; not usually in the surf, but more upriver, where the water is murky and in the dimness a paddling dog looks like something that a shark would like to eat.

But the sharks that eat them are not white pointers, which are an oceanic species. They are almost certainly bull whalers that swim far into the upper reaches of estuaries in search of a quick snack.

So where is all this leading us? Let me explain. What I'm trying to say is that sea creatures don't usually eat anything out of their environment and the bullock's blood myth is a classic example. But, as I said earlier, there are always exceptions.

One of the favourite all-time baits for bream is a mixture of cheese, salami and bread dough, all kneaded up into a 'pudding' mix and stuck onto the hook, rather than threaded on. Not much else except the bream will touch it and I can only wonder where the hell a bream would acquire a taste for such a concoction or, worse still, who was the inventor.

If you had just been sentenced to 10 terms of life imprisonment and you had all that time to come up with a ridiculous bait for bream, you still couldn't contrive that one during all those years in jail, so whoever first put it together is one bizarre individual.

Bream are also suckers for a bit of rump steak, and I can recall times in my youth when they wouldn't touch anything else. Mum used to go

MENU
1/4 POUNDER WITH BONES & FEATHERS
CRAPBURGER WITH CORN & CARROTS
LEG-ON-A-STICK
BATTERED BUMS
DAGWOOD DOGS (THE REAL THING)
SCRAPS

berserk when she'd get home and that night's roast was gone from the fridge, but we usually brought home a feed of fish which more than compensated.

We never stopped to wonder why those bream in Perth's Swan River would prefer the unnatural red meat to fish strips and prawns. It wasn't until years later that I realised that we used to fish just upstream from the Acme Smallgoods factory, and while we never actually saw the waste meat being pumped into the river through the outlet pipes, we certainly found plenty in the breams' stomachs when we cleaned them after the day's fishing. So that explained that.

But it doesn't explain how some trout prefer kernels of corn to juicy grasshoppers. Now here's a worry; who was the person who first put corn on a hook and discovered that the trout can't help themselves?

And while on the subject of strange things catching fish, it's interesting to note that the most successful trolling lure ever made is the humble Japanese feather jig made from — you guessed it — chicken feathers.

But this little bit of oriental ingenuity is self-explanatory. Just in case you're thinking that the tailor, salmon, kingfish, mackerel, tuna and other creatures that maraud on the surface are into a bit of tail-feather, think again.

The fact that the lure is made of feathers has a lot to do with its success, but only because when pulled at any sort of speed behind a boat, the feathers tuck in behind the metal head and flatten out to resemble a scurrying bait fish, most likely a pilchard, whitebait or bluebait or a garfish, to a pursuing predator.

And while the king of a country is supposed to be the cleverest of them all, the same cannot be said about his counterpart in the fish world, the street-fighting kingfish — they are the greatest dopes in the ocean, and one of their favourite snacks is metal . . . chromed metal, to be precise.

Kingies and their almost identical closest relative, the sampson fish, are total boofheads when it comes to munching on something that they shouldn't be munching, like chromed metal jigs. Well, maybe it's not that they shouldn't, it's more that you wouldn't expect them to.

The rules in Kingfishville are that if one does it, then it's okay for all of them to do it. Just like lemmings. One jumps off the cliff and the other wombats follow. For this reason it is easier to catch kingfish by dropping a flashing metal lure down into their domain, be it a reef or an undersea mountain. Wind and drop it at a rapid pace until one of the drongos eats it and all of the others will do the same the next time the lure comes back down.

It's called jigging or, if you're doing it way offshore, deep-jigging, and the kingies are suckers for it every time. Albert Einsteins in the last life they were not. Obviously the kingies see the tumbling flashing lures as something that they are likely to eat, like a wounded bait fish, and they go for it.

Considering that most modern lures are made of either wood or plastic, and olden-day lures were made from bone, it's not hard to realise that fish aren't real fussy when it comes to eating.

In the circumstances that led to what became known as the Shark Arm Murder in 1935, a captured tiger shark chundered up a human arm.

So let's look at the assortment of tasty tidbits. Dogs, animal meat, cheese, salami, dough, whole humans, metal, chicken feathers, wood, plastic, corn and human parts.

And some of you folks out there have the hide to think fish are smart. The wily old bream. The cunning old kingie. As smart as a marlin.

I don't think so. Just keep catching 'em and letting 'em go.

Anything that silly deserves to be caught more than once.

Sir Adrian's Record

This story is widely accepted as true and is oft repeated in legal circles. It was first told by Sir Adrian himself, one night when he was pissed, and he deeply regrets telling it. The names have been changed for obvious reasons.

Chief Magistrate Sir Adrian Farrington-Roycroft, OBE, was over the moon. The first day out on his brand new game-fishing boat *Quay Witness* and he had christened it with a whopper blue marlin — his first. And to top it all off, it could be an Australian record.

He held his breath as the huge fish was hauled up on the scales.

The crowd gasped as the weighmaster called it . . . '238 kilograms on 15 kilogram line. Congratulations, Sir Adrian. A new Australian record claim on 15 kilogram line.' He yelled it loud enough for the crowd to hear. Might as well slime the old prick, he thought to himself, you never know when you might have to front him on a drink-drive or other acts of antisocial behaviour involving alcohol. Sir Adrian was merciless on those.

Everyone adjourned to the bar of the Sydney Bluewater Fishing Club, where the drinks were on Sir Adrian. They all knew his reputation as a wowser, but today he surprised them all by his presence in a room where the dreaded drink was being served. And he was paying for it.

Sir Adrian's moral crusades were legendary. He made Mother Teresa look like Charles Manson. Everything that was halfway acceptable he hated . . . pornography, abortion, pot, prostitution . . . but most of all, alcohol.

It was this platform, along with a lot of arse-kissing, that had brought him to the pinnacle of his profession as the most respected district court judge in the country.

But Sir Adrian had a deep, dark secret: he was a closet pisshead. And a cunning one at that. Exposure could ruin him, so over the years he had developed a technique that allowed him to join in the fun without anyone being any the wiser.

He would wait until everyone around him was half flyblown, and then top his customary Coca-Cola up with scotch from one of his many hipflasks. By then the others would be so drunk that they never knew.

He saved his secret piss-ups for the right occasion — maybe a birthday or lodge night. And today was such an occasion: his first marlin and an Australian record to boot.

And so the festivities progressed into the night until Sir Adrian got paralytic and collapsed behind the big leather couch next to the trophy case.

When it was time to go, his fellow drinkers left him there. They felt it was not a good idea to wake him as he would then know they were onto him and he could make life difficult.

Instead, they moved him from full view and planned to say later that they couldn't see him anywhere, and thought he had snuck off home.

Of course he would agree that he had — 'couldn't stand all that boozing, you know!'.

Sir Adrian awoke to a dark, deserted clubhouse and turned on the lights. He found, to his horror, that he had chundered all over himself.

He looked like a mobile pizza and smelled like a brewery horse's farts. At least he had sobered up. But what to do? He wandered up the road and eventually hailed a cab that would take him as he was.

On the way to his city penthouse he plotted his excuse for the dreaded Lady Farrington-Roycroft, the Methodist minister's daughter he had been stuck with for the past 40 years.

He figured she suspected he had the odd nip, but even after all those years together she had never been able to prove anything.

But tonight would be the ultimate test.

'Sorry I'm late, darling,' he purred as the dragon came to the door, curious as to his whereabouts.

'Had a bit of drama on the way home.'

AXI

'Really,' she said suspiciously.

He explained about the big fish and shouting for the bar.

The old python growled at the thought of wasting their good money on the demon drink.

He then told her that the chap offering him a lift home appeared a little intoxicated and, rather than be put in a compromising position should they be pulled over, he had elected to leave early and catch a cab.

'Coming down Oxford Steet,' he explained, 'we were stopped at the lights when this drunk lunged at the cab, put his head in the window and vomited all over me,' he said.

'Fortunately the cab driver recognised me, apprehended the drunk and the police have him locked up at Darlinghurst police station. I've arranged that he comes before me tomorrow and I'm going to give him three months in Long Bay Gaol.

'Now, my darling, do you mind if I get out of these filthy clothes and go to bed? I'm absolutely exhausted after catching that huge fish.'

She smiled proudly at her husband and prepared a hot bath for him.

The following morning Sir Adrian was resting in his chambers nursing a monumental hangover when the phone rang. It was Lady Farrington-Roycroft.

'Sir Adrian,' she chortled. 'Remember that drunk who vomited all over you last night? What are you going to do about him?'

'They're bringing him up from the cells right now,' he replied. 'He appears before me at 10am and I'm going to give him three months in the Bay.'

'Well, you'd better make it six,' she said, 'because he shit in your underpants, too!'

The Fishermen Aren't Biting

Among the many stories that have become fishing folklore, this is one of the most famous, and there are many versions of it. This is the true story told in its entirety. Don't believe the other versions.

We christened him 'Spewie' because he was always going to 'bring it up' at the next meeting. Naturally, when his son was born we called him 'Chuck'. To this day, I doubt that anyone except the paymaster knew their real names.

Spewie was a tally clerk on the wharves and when Chuck was old enough to leave school he followed the family tradition and went to work on the docks.

They were inseparable, and as Chuck grew into manhood he'd join his old man at the pub a few times a week, and they'd get as full as Elle Macpherson's dance card.

Their downfall was that they loved a stink. They would fight anyone. Father and son would stand back to back and belt the shit out of anyone silly enough to stand up to them, then stagger over the pile of bleeding corpses and, arm-in-arm, sing their way home.

One night they met their match. They were pissed and started giving a bad time to a couple of guys at the bar. It was a big mistake. They were two bouncers from the illegal casino and they were used to belting a dozen yobbos a night.

The thrashing was sickening. The bouncers broke every bone in Spewie's and Chuck's bodies and kicked out every tooth in their heads.

When Spewie and Chuck got out of hospital several months later, their fighting days were over. They decided on a far less dangerous pastime — fishing. They bought a half-cabin boat and spent afternoons and weekends in the harbour catching tailor, flathead, trevally and bream.

They could drink to their hearts' content and catch a feed into the bargain. Life was great.

After a while they became more adventurous and ventured past the heads and out into the blue water in search of bigger fish.

It was only then that they discovered that Spewie was aptly named. Every time they went out wide of land, he got crook. He simply couldn't help himself. Every fishing trip off land he would hang his head over the side and have the most monumental chunder.

Chuck would sympathise with his father by consoling him and taking care of his expensive fangs, upper and lower — a legacy of 'that night' that they never spoke about.

It was a pitiful sight: Dad over the side, gormless, having the giant up-and-under, with his son standing dutifully behind with a handful of bodgie choppers.

Over the years things eventually got a little easier. At least Spewie wouldn't throw up on the way out. But the minute the boat was moored up, he was off, head over the side and calling for his friends Ruuuth, Raaalph and Berrrt.

But by now it was controlled. Once he had given in to the dreaded mal de mer and emptied the contents of his stomach, he was OK. He would retrieve his Jack Langs from Chuck, shoot 'em back in his gob and they would settle down to a good day's fishing and drinking.

This day Spewie was seriously crook. He'd had a skinfull of the dreaded pen and ink (casket red wine, to be precise) the night before, and the monumental hangover, combined with the engine fumes and the motion of the boat, saw to it that he was feeling very gravely butcher's hook.

And he looked it. His eyes were glazed and watery, his cheeks red and flushed and the colour of his tongue made it look as if he'd just kissed a vulture. And his breath could have put out a bushfire on the *Oriana*.

Nope, Spewie hadn't brushed up at all well on that fateful day.

A split second after they'd moored up at the Twelve Mile Reef,

Spewie felt the first savage rush coming through his body and headed for the side for the chunder of the century. If spewing was an Olympic event, he would have been the first athlete in history to win gold, silver and bronze . . . in the one event! It was a chunder of classic proportions. A projectile vomit that hit the water a good two metres from the boat.

Chuck patted his dad's head: 'You'll be right, mate. Just get it over and done with and let's do some fishing.'

His dad lifted his head to speak but was drawn back to the water by another incredible rush that started at his toenails . . . by the time it came out of his mouth, his whole body was quivering from the impact.

After Spewie had roared like a wounded bear and heaved into the next postcode, he lifted his head to say something, but was overcome once more with nausea.

'I know, Dad. You're trying to tell me you're OK,' Chuck purred.

'Fuckin' bullshit,' screamed his old man, determined to get the words out between heaves. 'I've just spat me fuckin' Jack Langs. I forgot to take the bastards out before I got crook. Now every fang in me fuckin' head's on the bottom of the fuckin' ocean with the shark shit.'

Chuck soothed his father and persuaded him to wash his mouth out with a nice, cold beer. After a couple more, Spewie accepted the fact that his choppers were gone for good. After a couple more he even had a giggle about it. They decided to fish on.

And as if Neptune was offering a fair swap, the snapper came on the bite. They loaded the boat with whopper reddies — great big 'old man' fish with huge bumps on their heads. It was their best day ever. They couldn't believe their luck.

It was just on dusk as they wearied of catching the huge fish and decided to leave them biting. Spewie steered while Chuck cleaned the catch on the way home.

'Dad,' Chuck yelled, 'look at this!' In the dark he produced a set of blood-soaked dentures from a snapper's stomach. More fossicking produced the other half. 'Christ, Dad, you wouldn't read about it,'

Chuck chortled. 'This bastard swallowed your dentures, both of 'em, and we caught him. You wouldn't believe it!'

His father was amazed. 'Gimme those,' he growled suspiciously. 'Let me wash 'em before I put 'em back in me gob.'

Spewie disappeared to the back of the boat. Chuck could hear the washing noises as his dad washed the slime and snapper gut off the dental plate with the contents of a can of beer.

Chuck couldn't control himself any longer and burst out laughing.

'Dad,' he chuckled. 'I'm sorry, I couldn't help myself. I played a joke on you. They're my teeth. I hid them in the fish for a laugh. Can I have 'em back now?'

'Bit fuckin' late,' came the gummy reply. 'I tried the bastards on a couple of times and when they didn't fit I threw 'em overboard.'

The Big Bad Bull Shark

What is the most evil shark of them all? White pointer, tiger, mako? No it's none of those. It's the estuarine whaler shark known more commonly as the 'bull whaler', a vile man-eater that inhabits estuaries and can live in both fresh and salt water. The bull whaler shark stops at nothing and is common in Australian waters.

I've got a lot of time for sharks, and there's no way anyone could ever convince me that they deliberately seek out and eat humans. Trust me, they are not that smart. In fact, I believe that when a shark attacks a human being it is not intentional.

The lunatic fringe would have us believe that sharks swim up and down the coast looking for surfers and swimmers to eat. I believe this to be complete and utter rubbish. If you happen to be in the water with a tiger, whaler or white pointer shark and it's hungry, chances are it will bite you.

But they don't kill humans just for the sake of it.

Having caught almost every species of shark available in our waters and been witness to many other captures, I thought I had a fair knowledge of our finned friends. But something always puzzled me. Up until a few years ago, that is.

As a boy growing up in Perth, I was always intrigued by the newspaper reports of dogs and horses being attacked by sharks in the upper reaches of the Swan River, about 20 to 30 miles from the ocean. The swimming dogs would disappear without a yelp and racehorses, being swum in the Swan River as part of their training, would often get nipped by mysterious aquatic assailants.

I always thought sharks were creatures of the sea, and I pondered just what species this might be — a shark that haunted estuaries and rivers. But I didn't lose any sleep over it. I accepted what the experts said: they were either small tigers or whalers.

The same year that I came to live in Sydney, 1963, a 32-year-old Sydney actress, Marcia Hathaway, died in hospital after being savagely bitten about the legs by an unidentified shark. The attack occurred at Sugarloaf Bay in Middle Harbour, a good way inside Sydney Heads.

But the most horrifying thing about it was that Miss Hathaway had been attacked in a mere 75 centimetres of water. This shark was so brazen and vicious that it left the experts dumbfounded.

There were various theories, the most common being that it was an over-protective tiger shark guarding her baby sharks. But no theory was ever proven conclusively.

Over the years, dogs kept disappearing, and people reported sightings of sharks upriver of Sydney Harbour, many, many miles from the sea. I always believed them to be small whalers, as we had caught a heap of them in the Hawkesbury River. They were savage and aggressive fighters, with teeth sharp enough to inflict terrible wounds.

Well, I was right . . . and I was wrong. After reading *Sharks and Rays of Australia,* by scientists Dr PR Last and Dr JD Stephens of the CSIRO Division of Fisheries, I have solved the mystery, perhaps not in all instances, but almost certainly in most of them.

Believe it or not, there is a shark in the book which is described by the good doctors as 'a very dangerous shark, perhaps more so than the tiger or even the white pointer, because of its extremely aggressive nature, powerful jaws, broad diet, abundance, and its preference for shallow, in-shore habitats'.

More dangerous than the tiger and the white? Holy mackerel! That's a big statement. They refer to this charming bit of work as the 'bull shark', which seems to be a very appropriate name but, unfortunately, leaves room for plenty of sensationalising by the scaremongers.

A brief summary of the bull shark tells it all. A member of the whaler family; known also as a river whaler; probably responsible for many attacks in and around Sydney Harbour; eats turtles, birds, dolphins, mammals and crustaceans (crabs and other shellfish) and molluscs.

The bull shark is found on most warm-water continents throughout the world and wreaks havoc in Australia from Perth all the way around the top to as far down the coast as Sydney. The bull shark has been found 4000 kilometres from the sea in the Amazon River system and, incredibly, can adjust easily to fresh water.

And just when you thought it was safe to go back in the water, the bull shark has been reported in numerous freshwater systems, including the Adelaide, Daly, East Alligator, Herbert, Brisbane and Clarence Rivers, and Lake Macquarie in NSW.

There's just no escaping them. The bull shark is also found in the ocean, though it is a 'close-to-shore' species rather than a current wanderer like many other members of the oceanic whaler family. They grow to a length of three and a half metres, but few have ever been recorded as captured, probably due to the confusion between them and other more common whalers.

So now the rest of us know what the scientists have known for years. However, it has never been explained to us as clearly as it is in *Sharks and Rays of Australia.*

Contrary to popular belief, whaler sharks are responsible for more human deaths than all other species of sharks combined. This is because whalers are the most common sharks in the world and frequent the warmer waters, where most people go swimming.

Of the 49 species of whalers, 30 are found in Australian waters. Of these, the bronze, black and white tip and bull whalers are all proven man-eaters.

The tiger shark is a member of the whaler family but is usually classified under its own name when it comes to being named as a man-eater. The other of the four proven man-eaters are white pointers and blue sharks.

A couple of years back a bull whaler of around 300 kilograms, about three metres long, was caught in knee-deep water in Sydney's Rose Bay. The area is a popular spot for waders and bait-gatherers and it is highly likely that it would have taken a human if the opportunity presented itself.

And in early 1997 a rowing scull was tipped over at Haberfield, in the upper reaches of Sydney Harbour, and the sole lady occupant was thrown out. On examination back at the club they found a lot of teeth marks in the bottom of the scull, indicating that a shark had attacked it. Pretty scary stuff, if it's true.

In my opinion the scull hit the shark (no doubt a bull whaler) first, as the shark was lazing on the top, probably looking for a feed. It retaliated by nipping the hull.

Still, I could be wrong. If the bull whaler is capable of attacking racehorses in the Swan River, it is no doubt capable of attacking a canoe.

Whereas I have a lot of sympathy for offshore sharks, and I believe that we shouldn't go out there to kill them when they are doing no harm, I certainly don't believe the same of the estuarine bull whaler, which hangs out where humans hang out and intentionally hunts and kills in the human domain. I believe that every one of them should be killed on sight.

Personally, I'd no more swim in Sydney Harbour or the Swan River than fly to Mars. Not while I know that the man-eating bull whaler shark could be lurking nearby.

SeaDuced by a Reel Screamer

They say that dogs look like their masters . . . but does the same apply to boats? Does the name of a boat tell us anything about the character of the owner? Having spent most of my life freeloading on other folks' boats, I definitely believe that it does.

I think it was the late Dean Martin who said that he felt sorry for people who didn't drink because when they woke up in the morning they knew that was as good as they were going to feel all day.

The master of the one-liner, Martin was also supposed to have said, 'a boat is a hole in the water that you never stop pouring money into'. Never a truer word spoken, and that's the main reason I've never bought one.

Besides, I've never really had to have my own boat, because in my capacity as a fishing writer I get a million invitations a year to go out on someone or other's boat and write a story about it. And having accepted plenty of those invites, I've spent much of my adult life on other people's boats of all shapes and sizes, either in pursuit of fish, or just lazing around chewing on a cold can, a chicken leg and a homemade Caesar salad.

And having met plenty of boat owners, I'm absolutely certain of two things.

Firstly, a boat name is always a reflection of its owner's personality, providing, of course, that the owner named the boat in the first place or re-named the boat when he bought it. It would be hard to imagine Elizabeth Taylor buying a boat named *Virgin Girl* and not changing the name.

And secondly, the ancient mariner's myth that changing the existing name on a boat will bring bad luck is a load of seagull crap.

I've known fishing boats that have never brought a fish to scale until they have a new owner and a new name. The minute the owner sells it and the new bloke changes its name, out it goes and loads up with fish week in and week out.

On the other hand, I have known some pretty famous fishing boats that have changed hands, and the new owners have insisted on keeping the original name, hoping that some of the luck would continue on . . . and they've never caught a thing.

In the 1960s and '70s, one of Australia's most successful boats was Dr Frank Ritchie's 31-foot Bertram, *Overdraft.* It was so named because at the time he bought it, Frank had to stretch his budget to buy it.

It became one of the most famous game-fishing boats in the country, but failed to carry on its remarkable career when it was sold, name included.

Possibly the most famous boat in Australian fishing history is *Sea Baby,* originally skippered by the late George Bransford, as it pioneered the huge black marlin fishery off Cairns. The three skippers who have worked *Sea Baby* in her 30-year history have all had phenomenal success with the same name.

But people name boats for different reasons, some of them pretty bizarre. A mate of mine had a long and successful business association with Telstra. When they eventually bought him out for a large, undisclosed sum, he bought a luxury cruiser and named it *The Tardis*, after the telephone box in the TV series *Dr Who.*

Champion racing car driver Frank Matich bought an old police boat, turned it into an extremely successful game-fishing boat and renamed it *Le Fuzz*. So much for the name change myth. *Le Fuzz* went on to break just about every record in the book.

Divorce and promiscuity also seem to bring out the best in boat-namers.

There are luxury cruisers on Sydney Harbour named *She Got The House, The Other Woman, The Mistress, Sure Beats Home* and *SeaDucer*. On the other hand, there's a boat kicking around called

Lackanooky, obviously owned by someone who doesn't have much success with the ladies.

And you must have seen a boat named *Woftam* in your travels. After all, just about every second boat in Australia has got that name on it because it stands for '*Waste of Fuckin' Time and Money'*.

Similarly, there's the big game-fishing boat operating out of Cairns called *Snafu,* which stands for '*Situation Normal. All Fucked Up*'.

And then there are the obvious ones like *Reel Affair, Reel Screamer, Reel Easy and Reel Action*. The late Louis Ardilley named his succession of boats *Santiago*, after the South American city the old man could see the lights of at night as he fought his huge fish out of his tiny boat in the Ernest Hemingway classic *The Old Man And The Sea*. And just like the old man in the tale, Louis and his crew battled many huge fish into the night, only to lose them at the boat or have them taken by sharks.

Horse trainer Bart Cummings named his boat *Leilani* after the champion mare which won him many races, including a Caulfield Cup. My friend Fritz Schroeder couldn't resist renaming his boat *Cuckoo's Nest* after he (Fritz) won a Jack Nicholson look-alike competition.

The old saying that they call a boat 'she' because she always heads for the 'buoys' when she's launched, is evident in the naming of such famous boats as Zane Grey's *Alma G* and also the *Lady Doreen, Kitty Vain, Lady Lola and Norma Jean.*

Max Lawson's famous *Murrawolga* is an Aboriginal word meaning 'blue water', and Paul Caughlan's series of boats are all named *Kanahoee*, Hawaiian for 'canoe'. American adventurer Jerry Dunaway roams the oceans of the world in his 33-metre mothership *The Madam*. The 12-metre fishing boat he carries on her deck is appropriately named *The Hooker*.

Fish names and connotations (such as the prized marlin which are also referred to as billfish because of their long beak or 'bill') are very popular. *Kingfisher, Billfisher, Bill Collector, Marlan, Broadbill, Albacares, Yellowfin, Bluefin, Mako, Hammerhead* and *Marlin Blue* are just a few.

Mind you, *Broadbill* has never fished for, or caught a *Broadbill* swordfish, and *Marlin Blue* fishes the Great Barrier Reef exclusively for black marlin.

Other boat owners to capture the adventurous life at sea in their boat names. *Smuggler, Sea Venture, Rum Runner, Coastal Trader, Pacific Adventure, Cloud 9* and *The Sheriff* all come to mind as names creating illusion, romance and adventure.

But the doozie of them all must be the half-cabin cruiser I saw running around Sydney Harbour the other day named *The Titanic.* Maybe there was another meaning to the word, so I looked it up in the *Webster*'s. But no: it says: 'Gigantic, colossal. Also the name of a British passenger liner, supposedly unsinkable, that struck an iceberg and sank off the Grand Banks of Newfoundland on its first voyage in 1912. 1513 lives were lost.'

There's no way you could get me on that boat, and I'm not even superstitious! The first thing you would do if you bought that boat is change its name. It sends a cold chill up my spine thinking about it.

Skidmarks and the Judge

There is little doubt that a certain amount of cheating goes on in fishing competitions, but the characters in this true story were so blatant about it that to this day no one knows how they got away with it. The fact that two dopes with only half a brain between 'em could devise such a scheme is the most amazing part.

The State Fishing Titles were the ultimate event in club fishing championships, and to win any one of the major categories meant fishing immortality. This was the event where superstars were born and living legends in the fishing world, such as Clem 'Stumps' Hall and 'Three-fingered' Syd White, came into being.

Legend has it that Stumps was blitzing the trevally and tailor at the bottom of a 100-metre cliff in horrendous conditions when he was swept in by a huge wave. He hung onto a rock for almost ten hours before someone spotted him and a rescue helicopter arrived to pluck him out of the drink.

But they didn't arrive in time to save a few of his fingers, which had been cut off at the stumps by the razor-sharp barnacle and oyster shells on the rock. Hence the nickname.

But even after his near-death experience and being relieved of a few of his Manly Warringahs, Stumps' only concern was winning the coveted Champion Angler trophy, so he scaled down the face of the cliff in a force-ten gale, recovered his fish, and had them back at the weigh-in just in time to take out top honours.

So extraordinary was his achievement that they named the bar at the club after him, the clem 'Stumps' Hall Bar an honour beyond the wildest dreams of any club angler.

©B.E.B.97

Three Fingers wasn't so fortunate. His lifelong ambition was to catch the heaviest fish of the Titles and he had prepared his plan of attack a long, long way in advance. A year or so before the event, he coaxed a 10 kilogram blue groper out of its cave on a secluded headland, by sitting on the rocks for days on end, throwing tiny morsels to it in an effort to befriend it. Without fail he returned to the spot every day with tasty offerings, and within six months he had the groper, which by now weighed about 40 kilograms, almost eating out of his hand. A week before the Titles, and the groper would do anything that Syd commanded as long as he supplied more food for its now grossly obese carcass — it had bloated out to about 75 kilograms.

Syd's plan was simple. On the first day of the Titles he visited the groper and hand-fed it a whole five kilogram snapper from the markets, but this time it had a hook in it, attached to a 1000 kilogram breaking-strain trace, which in turn was connected to a 500 kilogram main line and a huge rod and one of those big old-fashioned revolving drum reels with huge handles and no anti-reverse. Most certainly not the kind of gear to be catching groper with, but then again, Syd wasn't exactly rocket-scientist material.

Once the unsuspecting groper had taken the snapper, Syd snuck off to a makeshift fighting chair he had built out of rocks about 100 metres from the water's edge and settled in to take up the slack line and drag the groper out of the water.

The theory was that one of two things would happen. He would catch the fish before it was aware of what was going on, or it would feel the hook, take off and more than likely break the line. He hadn't counted on a third alternative.

He slowly retrieved the slack line, and as soon as he felt some pressure, he leaned back into the fishing rod with all his might to set the hook. That's when his theories of what would happen jumped out the window. He didn't catch the groper and the line didn't break. Instead, the giant fishing reel began revolving backwards in a blur as the huge fish felt the resistance of the line, realised that something was drastically wrong and headed back to its cave at breakneck speed, dragging with it the rod and reel and a couple of Syd's fingers that had been unlucky enough to be in the way.

Even though he didn't win the Biggest Fish trophy, Syd gained legend status with that little episode, and it's obvious that he would rather hear the story about himself told over and over again than have his fingers back.

Which leads me to the tale of Skidmarks and The Judge, and how they won the famed Doubles Event — the most coveted trophy of them all. The rules of the State Titles were simple. The most fish caught won on total weight. There were no boundaries and no line classes. Just catch-and-kill fishing. The only hard and fast rule was that berleying before the event was definitely not allowed as it would give the berleyers an unfair advantage. Outside of that it was open slather.

Skidmarks and The Judge were a couple of wharfies who were desperate for a little fame and recognition and they figured that the only way they could do it was through fishing. Skidmarks got his nickname because he was always going to 'follow through' on everything at the next union meeting: 'Yeah, just leave it with me and I'll follow through on it for ya.' Of course he never did.

They called his mate The Judge because he worked on the wharves but spent all his time sitting on a case.

For their devious scheme they co-opted the services of Mirrors (I'll look into it for ya) Marsdon, another wharfie, who just so happened to live next-door to the Hearty Host pie factory and through a hole in the fence had access to the reject pie bin. And believe me, there were plenty of rejects.

Every night for three months prior to the State Titles, they loaded up Mirrors' gravy-dripping ute with the reject pies and dumped them off the cliffs at the Devil's Gorge, a fishing spot that had been abandoned years earlier because it was too dangerous. No one ever went there any more.

It took a couple of days for the first fish to show up and as soon as the word got out that there was a free feed on every night, every fish within a hundred kilometres, including marlin, sharks and tuna, was there with its mouth open. Come the day of the State Titles, the Devil's Gorge was wall-to-wall fish — they outnumbered the pies by about ten to one.

With the help of Mirrors (who wasn't even entered in the event), they filled the ute in no time, took it to the weigh-in, emptied it and returned for more. That pair of cheats cleaned up just about everything, including the coveted Doubles Event. They got biggest fish of most species, winning team and a host of other cash and prizes.

Everyone could smell a rat because that pair were so stupid that they would have trouble catching a bus, let alone a couple of truckloads of fish. But there wasn't a darn thing we could do about it.

Eventually the truth came out: they started mouthing off one night when they were elephant's trunk. And when I think about it, I do recall looking at their ute outside the club on the presentation night and not being able to understand why there were a hundred cats licking out the back of the ute and a dozen dogs licking the chassis.

I remember thinking at the time, 'That's funny. Dogs don't like fish.'

Mind-bending Marlin

The basic ingredient of sportfishing is for the angler to catch as big a fish as possible on the lightest possible line without breaking any of the rules. A fish weighing ten times the breaking strain of the line used is brilliant, 15 to 1 is extraordinary and 20 to 1 is mind-boggling. But there are some anglers out there who dare to go even further than that.

A few years back I watched a bloke catch a 350 pound black marlin on a 16 pound breaking-strain line and then let it go. That puts the fish weight to breaking strain of the line ratio at around 22 to 1. Mind-boggling stuff! That's the same breaking-strain line that I use for catching two kilogram salmon and tailor off the rocks.

But when you consider that the same guy caught a 720 pound black marlin on six kilogram line, that first catch pales into insignificance. This one is a weight-to-line ratio of 60 to 1, the equivalent of trying to hold an elephant on cotton! It's almost impossible to believe, but it's fair dinkum. I use six kilogram breaking-strain line on one kilogram bream and flathead.

How could an angler land such a heavy fish on such light line? How could someone catch the most elusive game fish of them all on a line that you and I used to catch flathead and bream? Skill? Luck? Being in the right place at the right time?

It's all of these things, and I'm going to tell you how they do it.

I have always known how they catch huge sharks on light line for world and Australian record claims. They bend, but never break, the rules to the limit.

In most cases, the poor old sharks, usually makos, whites or blues, are berleyed up to the back of the boat, and once the angler has determined that the fish could be big enough to be a new world record on a certain line class, they feed it a bait attached to a regulation game-fishing outfit that fits the bill.

As the International Game-fishing Association rule book states that the fish must be fought fairly, they usually prod the poor thing with a boathook so that it pisses off from the back of the boat, taking line with it as it goes. They then berley the shark back up to the back of the boat.

This is called 'fighting the fish' and manages to scrape through their loose interpretation of the rules.

Once it has been 'fought' back to the boat on denier-thin line, the crew whack a couple of flying gaffs in it and hang on for their lives.

The poor old shark doesn't know what hit it, and before long it's hanging up by its tail at a weigh station with some wanker standing alongside it telling everyone how clever he is and how he survived his brush with death.

What a crock of crap! So much for the great white hunters. These impostors make elephant poachers look like humanitarians.

Some of the shark records are bordering on the absurd. The late and great Bob 'Pappy' Dyer was the first one to admit that his 484.44 kilogram white shark on 10 kilogram line is a classic example. Can you imagine *fighting* a 1100 pound shark to a grinding halt on a 20 pound line? Give me a break.

But the record books are riddled with these examples and no doubt those records will still be standing long after they have laid me to rest.

But while sharks are gullible enough to swim up to the back of a boat to be hand-fed, the marlin and tuna are not, so they must be hooked in a different manner.

I doubt that anyone in the world would know more about catching huge fish on minuscule line than the famous American angler, Mike Levitt.

On my annual trip to Cairns several years ago, I was lucky enough to spend a day on *Sea Baby II*, skippered by Captain Paul Whelan, and watch Mike in action with his two hot deckies, Charles (CP) Perry and local hot-shot Bob Forbes.

As you're about to find out, the angler ain't got a prayer without a

good crew. Mike holds six world records for billfish, caught on one, two, four, six and eight kilogram line. He is the only man ever to catch an Atlantic sailfish and a black marlin on a two kilogram breaking-strain line that you and I could snap with our bare hands.

So how do they do it? Simple. Outside the Great Barrier Reef, where the black marlin are as thick as the fleas on a cattle dog, the *Sea Baby* trolls baits around that have no hooks in them.

That's right . . . no hooks. Crazy? Why would anyone spend all that money to come to Australia and then an arm and a leg to charter the top light-tackle fishing act in the world, to drag baits around without any hooks in them?

Well, the baits are really 'teasers' and once a marlin rises to one of them and has a crack at it, it (the marlin) can't get hooked up. That's when they drive the poor fish nuts by dragging the bait away and 'teasing' it into coming up to the back of the boat.

I saw one marlin get really pissed off. Every time it got the whole tuna bait in its cavernous mouth, one of the boys would drag the hookless bait away, leaving the marlin scratching its head and wondering what happened to lunch. It would then zero in on the other bait, and that too would be dragged away. They kept it up until they had 'teased' the fish so close to the back of the boat that they could have reached over and patted it.

By now Mike had had a good look at the fish and decided what line class he would feed it. In this case the fish was about 175 kilograms and he decided to catch it on eight kilogram line. So when the fish was going apeshit at the back of the boat, darting this way and that in sheer frustration and ready to eat anything put in front of it, Mike presented it with a bait with a hook in it, which it wolfed down.

Once the fish felt the resistance of the line and realised that something was amiss, it was off like a bride's nightie and the *Sea Baby* was in hot pursuit backwards. As he was playing the marlin, Mike explained to me that providing the fish stayed on top, they would have a chance of catching it.

If it took off into the bottomless abyss off the continental shelf, they had no hope on such light tackle.

But stay on top it did. It jumped many times, and each time it did, the crew breathed a sigh of relief that it didn't land on the spider's-web-thin line. After an hour it was sitting on the surface about 100 metres away and Captain Whelan decided to have a crack at getting it.

He gunned *Sea Baby* backwards and Mike wound line as fast as his arms allowed. They were on top of the fish before it knew what was going on. CP had the trace in his hand and took a couple of wraps and hung on while Bob stuck a numbered tag in the bewildered marlin, then cut the thick nylon trace and let it go.

They could have killed the fish and boasted of their conquest, but they chose to let it go. Imagine that. Letting a 175 kilogram fish on eight kilogram line go. In anyone's book it would be the catch of a lifetime. But not these guys.

To them the super-abnormal is all in a day's fishing.

And they reckon it's easy when you know how.

The Last of the Shark Hunters

I grew up and fished with most of the old-timers and listened in awe to their stories of great sea creatures and how they went about catching and killing them. My friend Stewart Donaldson is one of those wonderful characters who now spends his time preaching conservation of the oceans rather than killing.

He's getting on a bit now, the old shark hunter. But at 84, Stewart Donaldson's memory is a sharp as ever and he recalls epic battles with mammoth sea monsters as if they had taken place yesterday.

Stewie tells tales of huge sharks that defy the imagination, totally fearless as they glide up the berley trail and rip and tear at the slabs of whale blubber hanging from the side of the boat.

Giant-toothed critters with mouths the size of 44-gallon drums that could straighten tempered steel hooks and swallow two men at a time. Cruising cannibals that would eat their brethren at the drop of a hat and have even been known to eat their own entrails.

To the last of the old shark hunters, it was all in a day's sport. Stewie is one of the few survivors of those days in the '50s when it wasn't frowned on to use whale blubber as berley and bait to attract and catch the sharks that the public hated so much.

Rather than being the anti-conservationists and murderers they would be labelled today, shark hunters of that era were seen as heroes, and the newsreels and press loved them.

Bob and Dolly Dyer, Alf Dean, Charlie Chambers, Jack Davey, Errol Bullen and Max Lawson were household names. With the exception of Dolly, who lives in retirement on the Gold Coast, they've all gone now, and all Stewie has left are the memories and the scrapbooks.

'In those days there were thousands of humpback whales in a never-ending procession going past Brisbane's Moreton Bay about a quarter of a mile offshore', he recalls. 'We just assumed they were there for the whale chasers to kill and then their parts would be used to make oil, soap and even perfumes.

'Whaling was big business, and at Tangalooma whaling station on Moreton Island they would carve up the carcasses, and the blood and offal would be hosed into Moreton Bay.

'It was like whistling in the cows. Sharks would turn up in their thousands — whalers, tigers and giant white pointers — and it was on for young and old as they fought for the scraps.

'You could have walked to the whaling station on their backs, and we used to part them with the boat as we called into get some blubber for berley and bait.

'There was no thought that anyone could be doing the wrong thing by killing the whales, and even less thought for the sharks that were killed in their thousands by amateur anglers in the name of sport. In fact, Bob Dyer had shares in the whaling industry.'

From Forestville, in New South Wales, Stewart spent most of his early years fishing around Sydney for blackfish. He always had a fascination for sharks and read everything he could find about them. It was this knowledge that got him on to the shark boats in the first place.

'I was at Watsons Bay one Sunday watching Bob Dyer weigh a few sharks he'd caught off Sydney,' he recalls. 'The joint was lousy with 'em in those days and I said to Dyer's boatman, Basil Davidson, "That's a nice couple of bronze whalers and a tiger".'

'Basil was surprised at my textbook knowledge of sharks and told me that the famous fisherman of the day, Max Lawson, was looking for a crewman. I rang Max, got the job and fished out of Sydney with him on Thursdays, Saturdays and Sundays.

'We caught every type of shark imaginable . . . tigers, makos,

whalers, white pointers, hammerheads, and other game-fish such as marlin and tuna,' Stewart says.

'But all the publicity was coming out of Moreton Bay, where Dyer was bringing in up to 10 sharks a day and catching white pointers weighing over 900 kilograms. We decided to go up and take a look.

'Four of us took all our fishing gear, chartered a 20-metre trawler out of Moreton Bay and moored for a week at a time at Yellow Patch, on the tip of Moreton Island, in 15 metres of water. The fishing was unbelievable — thousands of sharks, and any amount of huge snapper and kingfish hovering underneath them.

'We hung huge pieces of blubber on ropes on the sides of the boat. As the rocking dipped them in and out of the water, huge tigers and whites would compete to bite them. In order to beat the others to it, the white pointers would come head and shoulders out of the water to get at it first. That was a very scary sight.

'The whites were the cheekiest of the lot. I remember one day Dick Rowe was handlining for snapper when a huge white pointer launched itself in through the tuck at the back of the boat and almost grabbed him by the legs. Dick went the colour of the yellow spray jacket he was wearing, and I don't blame him.'

While thousands of sharks in the area offered sport all day long, Stewie says it was the white pointers that were hunted the most.

'The world-famous angler Zane Grey had christened them "the great white death". Public interest was aroused and the more we killed and strung up on the gantry, the more people turned out to herald us as heroes.

'We could bring in tigers and whalers up to 500 kilograms, but they wanted to see the huge whites. And they were nasty bastards of things. One day I caught a 400 kilogram whaler and had it hanging off the side of the boat when a monster white came along and ate it in three bites. And the whaler was still alive. That white would have been five metres long and weighed more than 1000 kilograms.

'At night we would try to sleep as the huge whites bashed against the boat, gorging themselves on the carcasses of tigers and whalers we had hanging off the side.'

And how does the old man of the sea feel about the killing of sharks and whales these days?

'I have no regret about what we did in those times,' he says. 'There were plenty of sharks and whales around and they were there for the killing. That was how we were brought up.

'But these days I'm against the killing, because if we continue the way we are, there will be no great sea creatures left. The difference in what's out there now, compared to what we used to see only 40 years ago, is astonishing. And if it's allowed to go on, in another 40 years there will be nothing.

'Yes, the killings had to stop,' he says.

And the last of the old shark hunters would know better than anyone.

Author's note:

Stewie Donaldson passed away in September, 1997, after the stories in this book had been completed. As requested by Stewie before he died, I delivered his eulogy and read excerpts from the next story in this book, 'The Day of the Great White Death', which involved him.

The last of the old shark hunters is at rest.

The Day of the Great White Death

These days very few huge white pointer sharks are killed by recreational anglers. In fact, in some Australian states it is illegal to fish for them. But in bygone days they were regarded as the enemy and brave men and women put to sea to capture them and hang them up for all to see. This is one of their stories.

'Stewart, come quickly!' Grace Donaldson called to her husband. 'I think we're drifting onto a reef.' He was at her side in an instant. The dark shape beneath the boat brought back many memories. None of them good.

'That's no reef, Grace. That's a great white shark!' he exclaimed. Grace paled at the thought.

Next thing, the 'reef' was alongside the boat. It bit a 400 pound whaler hanging from the side in half with one bite.

Stewart had told his wife many stories of these mammoth fish that know no fear and are as cold-bloodedly casual as the deadliest of killers.

Now she looked death in the eye as the huge fish rolled and lunged at the remains of the stricken whaler. It lifted itself head and shoulders out of the water, a trick the whites use to snatch sleeping seals off the rocks in the southern waters. Another mouthful of whaler and the huge fish slid back below the surface.

Stewart Donaldson was no stranger to their arrogance. He recalled trying to sleep on board *Murrawolga* at Yellow Patch, Tangalooma, in Brisbane's Moreton Bay, years earlier. Sleep didn't come easy. All night the bumping of the great whites gorging on the captured sharks, tail roped to the side, kept them awake. Only a thin skin of marine ply kept them from certain death.

In the morning they would find the remains. All that was left of the enormous whalers and tigers was their tails hanging in the ropes. The feeding orgy over, the great whites would disappear as silently and gracefully as they arrived. Stewart and his fellow anglers had caught whites, gutted them and then watched as the fish ate their own entrails.

The Cape Moreton whaling station was operating then, and the area was a natural feeding ground for sharks. The fishermen would buy whale blubber and use it for berley. Moored up at Yellow Patch, the berley trail would attract visitors instantly. All sizes . . . all species.

Stewart had seen a white slide up the back of the boat to steal a morsel of whale meat from the bait board like a naughty dog stealing sausages from the back of a butcher's truck. Over the years his hatred for these most notorious of man-eaters had turned to respect.

Grace helped the men clear the deck, then took up residence in the cabin as the crew went to work. All lines were brought in and Charlie Chambers hurriedly baited a giant hook with the remains of the whaler's tail. He attached the wire trace to the huge rod and reel filled with 130 pound cord line and floated it out in the direction of the giant fish, now mooching around in the berley.

Bob Head took the wheel while Basil Davidson cleared the decks, ready for a hook-up. At first it appeared that the shark was not interested in the bait. It cruised past, heading back toward the boat, its huge dorsal fin cutting the chop.

Then, with one swish of its awesome tail, it did a full circle, and in a second it was on the bait, wolfing it down. Charlie let the big fish get the bait right down before he set the hook.

Strike!! The big diesels roared to life and the fight was on . . .

The events leading up to this started on Anzac Day 1956. The Max Lawson-owned *Murrawolga* was moored up on Long Reef Wide, northeast of Sydney Heads. Max was marching in the Anzac Day parade, so the crew headed out without him.

Basil Davidson had taken the first strike — a whaler of 450 pounds. Basil again drew the short straw and soon another larger whaler was tied alongside. Bob Head was next in the chair. Yet another big whaler. Non-stop action now as Stewart Donaldson soon had an out-of-season marlin of 85 kilograms secured to the bollard.

Then quiet. The baits remained untouched for an hour. The men drank beer and played cards in the cabin while Grace Donaldson handlined for snapper . . . until Mr Big arrived . . .

Charlie leaned back into the huge split-cane rod. The sheer bulk of the predator had him in awe. The fish was very aware that something was wrong, and showed it by first rolling up in the trace and then thrashing around near the surface. Then it took off on a series of long runs that had smoke pouring from the Hardy reel. The crew cooled the angler and the reel with buckets of water.

For an hour the fish doggedly headed east, with the *Murrawolga* in hot pursuit, gaining line at every opportunity. Just when they thought the fight was over, the fish would head off again, peeling line from the reel whenever it desired. The cuttyhunk cord held.

Charlie knew his trade well. Not once was the pressure taken off the fish. Each time it looked like taking more line than necessary the angler leaned back hard on the thick rod to let his adversary know who was to dictate the terms. Several times they feared the shark lost as it entangled itself in the trace and rolled on the line. But each time the line miraculously came out unscathed.

One hour and 40 minutes of backbreaking struggle had the fish at the side of the boat.

'Basil's on the wire . . . You're first gaff, Stewie,' Charlie commanded.

Basil's thickly gloved hands wrapped the wire as Bob reversed the boat towards the fish.

Stewart reached out across the shark's width to secure the vital first gaff, but the immense girth of the fish would not allow it to make the distance and the sharp point kept skidding off its back.

'It's just too big, Charlie,' Stewart called. 'We'll have to risk a mouth gaff.'

Charlie leapt from the chair and disconnected the flying head of the gaff from the handle. Poised near the snapping jaws, he waited for the right moment to place it in the shark's mouth. Having done so,

Stewart pulled the rope taut and the giant gaff head penetrated the upper jaw.

'At least we've got one end of him secure,' Stewart called, 'but the other end isn't going to be that easy. That's the bit with the tail.'

The boat was taking a pounding as the massive tail thrashed and hammered at the gunwale. The crew were drenched. Charlie hung firm on the mouth gaff rope.

'Get another gaff in the mid-section if you can,' he called to Stewart. Stewie did so and the shot was good. The gaff went cleanly into the giant white's underbelly. Still the giant fish wreaked havoc. If something wasn't done quickly to bring it under control, the ropes would snap or the bollards would break.

At this stage the fish's head was securely tied halfway up the boat but its enormous length left the tail trailing six feet beyond the stern. Only a tail-rope would secure their prize.

'You're going to have to go over the side, Stewie,' Charlie grimaced. 'It's the only way we're going to get a rope around its tail.'

Under normal circumstances you would rather be stuck in a lift with Jack the Ripper than go over the side with that giant, very angry fish, but it was not the time for indecision.

Stewart was held by the feet and lowered out to the shark's tail. He floated the huge lasso around it and pulled tight. The fish was theirs. Another two tail-ropes and the battle was over.

They radioed to base that they were bringing in a huge shark. The word spread quickly. People turned out in their thousands to watch the weigh-in. It tipped the scales at 2100 pounds. That's just under 1000 kilograms!!

The great white shark was 16 feet and one inch long and 16 feet around the girth.

To this day it is the largest fish ever taken in New South Wales waters.

Charlie Chambers died in 1976. His ashes were scattered at Long Reef Wide.

The Bottle Shop Bargain

**Swap a fish for a few beers? No problem.
And this time I thought I'd got a real good deal.
But it didn't quite work out that way.**

The bloke at the local grog shop had been robbing me for years. But it suited me to go there, even though I knew I was paying five bucks more for a carton of beer than I would at the discounters. I could park right out the front — and he was always good for a chat.

Over the years I could have saved a fortune by going elsewhere, but we had become good mates and the money wasn't all that important.

I'd never really thought about getting even with him until a while back, when my young bloke Ben and I had just returned from a long day's fishing off Sydney and we called in for a carton of ice colds on the way home.

'Been fishin', boys?' the old burglar asked us. 'You look as though you might have caught something.'

And we had. But not what we wanted. We had gone out with Captain Ross Hunter on his charter boat *Broadbill*, hoping to get big yellowfin and albacore tuna, but all we managed to catch was a boatload of striped tuna, or skipjack tuna, as they are known in some states.

The stripies were up around the five kilogram mark and great fun to catch on three kilogram and six kilogram line, but they were a blood tuna with rich, red flesh — lousy to eat, not like the delicious pink-fleshed albacore and yellowfin tuna.

As I'd promised about 500 people some tuna steaks, it had been a disappointing day.

Not all tuna are good eating and on a scale of one to 10, the poor old stripey would pull a zero. However, the Greeks and Italians love it,

GROGAN'S GROG
Liquorium 'n' Boozer
DRIVE IN...WALK, SHUFFLE, CRAWL
THIS WEEK'S Specials
RUFF RED LEGGO FOR DOGS $3.99
STARWINE (COLLECTORS VINTAGE) 55¢ BUCKET
RUBY PORT VINTAGE 7 AM TODAY $1.00 GRAM
METHYLATED COGNAC FREE TO OUR REGULARS
NEW 'MUDWEIN' YARRA VALLEY BROWN MUSCAT
FRESH BATTERY ACID DAILY
BLACK & GREEN OIRISH SCOTCH
NO CREDIT GIVEN TAKE IT OR NUTHIN
HIGH KLARSS LEGGO
$!
SOMEONE SURE GOT CONNED, EH...
KIN I HAVE A TINNY, POP?
FISH N KIDS

because they know how to marinate and cook it in oil and spices and disguise the rich, bloody flavour.

Anyway, back to the plot. As disappointed as we were at not catching some eating fish, I had still snookered a couple of good-sized stripeys for our three cats. They loved it and they would save me a fortune in canned food over the next couple of weeks.

Besides, I love the way the cats react when I plonk a whole tuna across their bowl. They flick their tails and parade around the poor old stripey as they take jabs at it with their claws before they tear bits off it and eat them. It's like a ritual.

So when my thieving friend at the bottle shop inquired as to the day's results, I casually answered . . . 'Yeah. We didn't do too bad. Just a whole heap of tuna.'

'Tuna!' he exclaimed. 'You're kidding. My wife loves tuna.'

I stopped dead in my tracks. The only tuna he would ever have had would have been the white-fleshed variety from the markets. He assumed they all tasted the same. And to him they all *looked* the same.

I decided to do him a deal on the stripey. And if he started to grizzle and whinge later on that it tasted lousy and made his kids crook, then I would say it must have been the way he cooked it.

I explained that I had only brought a couple home and they were promised. By now he was pleading.

I winked at Ben who joined me in the con and begged me not to give one away, on the pretext that he wanted to show his mates what he had caught.

'Besides,' I lied, 'they're $20 a kilo at the markets at the moment,' knowing full well that he wouldn't know it was the yellowfin and albacore that were bringing the big bucks. If stripey ever made it to the markets it would be lucky to bring a dollar a kilo.

'I'll swap you a case of beer for one,' he said, tumbling into us at a million miles an hour. We had him.

'No, Dad,' Ben protested. 'They're my fish. I caught them. You can't do it to me.'

The more Ben looked distressed, the more the old shafter was determined to get one of those tuna.

Brushing Ben aside, I begrudgingly swapped the stripey for a case of beer, assuring him all the time that he had come out on top.

Ben's whingeing turned to shrieks of laughter as we walked out of earshot with our free case of beer.

'Got him,' I said to my son. 'I can't wait to see the look on his face when he tells us what it tasted like.'

The following day curiosity got the better of us and we fronted up at the liquor store.

'How was the fish?' I inquired. 'I haven't had it yet,' he said. 'My wife is preparing it for tonight and we'll have some friends over for a barbecue.'

Yuk. Barbecued stripey. What a horrible thought. I nearly threw up. And he was going to feed it to his friends!

I felt like warning him, but the joke had gone too far. The next day curiosity got the better of us again.

Half-expecting him to hit me over the head with an empty wine bottle for embarrassing him and his family in front of their toffy friends who had come over for a whoop-up tuna treat, I asked, 'How was the fish?'

'It was sensational,' he said. 'Best bit of fish we've ever eaten. I'll take as many of those as you can catch.'

I was dumbfounded. No one could eat stripey and enjoy it. Except my greedy cats.

Admittedly, I had my case of beer and I was a mile in front, but my joke had backfired.

Maybe I had been wrong about stripeys.

Out of curiosity we barbecued one. It was absolutely dreadful.

A week later I called in again. The old scoundrel was not to be seen.

'Dad's on holiday,' his daughter told me.

I couldn't help myself. 'Did you really enjoy that fish?' I asked, desperate to know.

'You mean that tuna?' she replied. 'Hell no, Dad didn't eat it. He sold it to the Italian guy next-door for $80. He hasn't stopped laughing since.'

Flies, Like Martinis, Should be Dry

Have you ever wondered why the folks who fly-fish are generally regarded as a bunch of snobs by the blue-water brigade? It's probably because a vast percentage of them are. And lots of them make no bones about their elitist pastime and its upper-class ancestry.

Until recent years, I had always reckoned that most of the fly-fishing fraternity were a bunch of elitist snobs. To my mind, they tried to give the impression that they were better than anyone else and that their chosen form of fishing was much more difficult than all the other forms of angling put together.

The 'gentleman's sport', I think they call it. Something that could be likened to fox-hunting, rugby and rowing. Strictly for the old-school-tie brigade.

But just because I think like that, it doesn't necessarily mean that I'm right. Far from it.

Lots of blokes I know these days who go fly-fishing certainly wouldn't fit into that category.

I'm sure Rex Hunt, Steve Starling, Bushy, Garry McDonald and Charles Wooley wouldn't like to be classed as toffs, and they are all fanatical fly-fishers.

And, as blokes, you couldn't meet a more down-to-earth bunch. There's certainly no old school tie about any of them.

I can assure you there are plenty of ordinary blokes and women out there getting into fly-fishing without all of the pomp and crap that used to go with it.

I doubt you would find Charlie or Rex wandering around a lake or

...CHAPS

MAJOR
MAJOR

a mountain stream in a velvet jacket with leather elbows and sporting a cravat.

And as some of the fellows casting handmade artificial enticements at the rainbows and browns these days aren't wearing that old traditional clobber, does this mean that one of the oldest forms of angling is conforming to today's standards?

What a ghastly suggestion, old boy. Heaven forbid!

But, even with today's fly-fishers being a little less rigid, why do I always associate them with ancient ports and whiskys and old money? I've asked myself this question often.

And why would I bother wasting my time thinking about the trouties, anyway? It all has to do with my job as a fishing writer: fly-fishing is becoming more and more a part of what I write about. So I might as well come to terms with the diggers who do it.

Maybe it's the tradition of dry fly-fishing that makes me think it's only for the snooty few — it dates back to the late eighteenth century and was the favoured pastime of kings of England and lords and knights of the realm.

I think that, to some, the trout is only a minuscule part of the art of fly-fishing. I think that to the would-be's, who are fortunately a dying breed, the sport is more about dress, social status and class values. And those old duffers are in it more for the bulldust value than anything else. Most of them are whisky-swilling old farts who get their kicks from sitting around in a gentleman's club pissing in each other's ears about the one that got away.

When it comes to snobbery, some of the exclusive fly-fishermen's clubs in Tasmania take the cake. So much so, that members refer to themselves as 'purists', in that they would never dream of using a bait or lure. They only use dry flies, the ones that float on the top and don't go under the water like those 'vulgar' wet flies that are the next best thing to bait.

They wear all the top clobber. Checked shirts and tartan ties. Leather-elbowed tweed jackets with matching hats covered in a variety of flies. Some of them stomp through the undergrowth in 'plus-fours' and brogues. And there is the inevitable hipflask and briar pipe.

A Tasmanian fly-fishing mate of mine, who prefers to remain nameless for fear of reprisals, tells of two members of a Tassie 'purists' club who were sprung bait-fishing for trout. It was a dull, overcast day when the trout weren't rising and they had obviously found a couple of their great-grandchildren's spinning rods in the boot of the Rover and baited them up with witchetty grubs for a bit of fun.

But they were sprung by one of the members hiding behind a nearby tree. I wouldn't even attempt to guess what he was doing there.

The pair were hauled before the committee and members at a special meeting and, in true British court-martial tradition, were found guilty of the most heinous of crimes — attempting to catch trout on bait.

They were made to stand in front of everyone while the president stripped their tweed hats off, broke their fly rods over his knee and sent them off into the night, banished for life, never to be seen again. Bloody good show, old chap. That'll teach them to try to enjoy themselves. How dare they!

Every time my mate tells me that story I picture them as a club full of old goats, all of whom look like the major out of *Fawlty Towers.* My nameless mate swears blind that it's a true story, and he has many more stories just like it to prove tradition is alive and well on the Apple Isle.

And my mate would know. After all, he's a true-blue Taswegian and proud of it, though he admits that some of the trouties go a tiny bit over the top.

But he is quick to add that you haven't lived until you've caught a trout on a dry (floating) fly.

So why is it that everyone associates dry fly-fishing for trout with the landed gentry and other assorted toffs? Even my wife, who knows about as much about fly-fishing as I know about wildebeest breeding, said she always thought of fly-fishers as a bunch of snobs.

There was only one way to find out. I rang my friend John Turnbull in Canberra. John is one of Australia's foremost authorities on trout, and has spent a lifetime writing articles and books about them, catching them and studying them. If anyone would know, it would be the old master himself.

'Wet fly-fishing goes back 2000 years,' John told me. 'The Roman historian Aurelius, who was a sort of travelling journalist of the times, described flies that are the equivalent of the Red Hackle fly which is still in use today. The Macedonians were fishing with flies about AD 260. But these were all wet flies. The dry fly was invented around the 1880s, after someone invented the rods to cast them with.

'The best fishing spots were in the south of England and France in the chalk streams. They were extremely fertile, as the dissolving nutrients would percolate through the chalk, providing lush weed growth that is the home of the plump insects that are the main food source of the trout. As these trout loved a feed of hatching insects, they often rose to feed on the surface. When they did, the only way to catch them was with a dry fly.

'As the best streams were on the best properties, which were owned by the rich squires, dry fly-fishing was a sport to be enjoyed only by the wealthy and their guests.

'And as that lot pranced around in ballgowns, wigs and satin suits, irrespective of whether they were having dinner, playing croquet or fishing, that's the way it is with some people even to this day.

'Even in those bygone times, the pretenders got to be somebody marvellous just by getting into dry fly-fishing. Amazing, but true. The silliest thing about this kerfuffle is the fact that trout are easiest to catch on the dry fly.'

Need I say more?

The Deaf Snapper

Fishing and villains seem to go hand in hand. Often fishing boats are used to pick up drug hauls out at sea and dispose of bodies. Mafia Godfather John Gotti operated out of New Jersey's Bergen Hunt and Fish Club. There's always a marlin or sailfish on the wall in a movie gangster's office. And Al Capone loved to fish. This is a gangster fishing story.

Back in the '60s, when Sir Robert Askin ruled the Sydney underworld from Parliament House, a card-carrying member of the underworld, Don Georgio Spilotro, lorded over his flourishing starting price gambling empire with a fist of tungsten and the wrath of a pissed-off pit bull terrier.

This was long before the days of the TAB, and the only way to get a bet on off the racecourse was through an illegal SP bookie. These were about as hard to find as a racehorse at Randwick.

And, in one way or another, Don Georgio controlled a large percentage of them, as he had the Premier's ear and saw to it that for a weekly consideration the police turned a blind eye to his SP bookies operating out of hotels, clubs and anywhere else the punter was likely to want to get set.

And they bet on anything . . . horse races, trots, dogs and even the 18-footer sailing races on Sydney Harbour.

Don Georgio was the most frightening human being I have ever laid eyes on. Tall and lean, athletically fit and immaculately groomed, Don Georgio looked considerably younger than his 50 years.

He had the swarthy, handsome, Ricardo Montalban, European-type looks that the women of the day swooned over, and sported a long, ugly scar that ran from just beneath his left eye, over which he wore a black eye-patch, to the corner of his mouth.

Legend had it that the young Georgio Spilotro picked up his facial souvenir some twenty-five years earlier in a knife fight to the death with the now very late Mick the Turk over control of Sydney's inner-city brothels.

The Turk was all over him when, with blood pouring from his punctured eyeball, Georgio took one last desperate lunge and slit the Turk's throat from ear to ear. He then sliced off his enemy's ears for souvenirs and pissed in the gaping throat wound in front of the spectators.

From that day on, no one ever messed with Georgio Spilotro. As he graduated from running whorehouses to the much more respectable business of SP gambling, the legend grew, and he was bestowed the honour of being titled Don Georgio by his peers.

Don Georgio wore his scar and eye-patch as badges of honour.

Stories of his methods of collecting from the unfortunates who had got in too deep or had taken the knock were legend throughout the Sydney underworld.

His favourite trick was to have his chief executioner, Chiller, hang a victim on a meat hook in the back of a refrigerated meat truck until the poor bastard either came good with the money or froze to death.

The Don had two favourite recreations. One was horning around Sydney Harbour in the summer months on his boat full of colourful characters, drinking French champagne, snorting cocaine and impressing an endless supply of topless beauties who queued up at the wharf in the hope that they might be invited out for a lavish day of sin and lust on the water.

But his real passion was fishing Sydney's offshore reefs for bottom species such as snapper and kingfish, though he never seemed to have much luck.

The Don had started out his boating career with a modest 25-foot Bertram and had moved up slowly through the years, ending up with his beloved 50-foot Chris Craft *Georgie Boy.*

And, like most men from humble beginnings, he adored his magnificent toy with a passion and kept it in mint condition.

Back in those days I fished with Keith Whitehead on his 35-foot Bertram, *Splashdown,* and every time we came back from fishing off Sydney Heads with a marlin or a shark dragging off the back of the boat and we passed the Don and his team on the harbour, Keith would wave to him. The Don would be standing in the cockpit, tanned and fit, cigar in one hand, champagne flute in the other, with a dozen topless to-die-for babes hanging off him and his cronies.

'How do you catch those things?' he asked Keith, pointing at the fish hanging off the back of the boat and ogling the big snapper we held up.

'I've been out there this morning and I've caught nothing. How come you bastards are so smart?'

Keith would wave back and say, 'It's the gear, Don Georgio. You've gotta have the right equipment. If you decked your boat out for fishing you'd catch more fish. It's as simple as that.'

Don Georgio's favourite of all of the girls at this time was a showgirl named Stella who was about as close to a permanent girlfriend as he would ever allow. Stella was a party girl who looked for all the world like Marilyn Monroe, but with black hair.

The Don used to take Stella out fishing with him and her enormous breasts and wiggling butt drove the other blokes on the boat nuts. Stella spent half her time pampering the boss and the other half getting her stiletto heels out of the gaps in the planks along the marina.

Whitehead had the agency for Chris Craft boats then, and had sold Don Georgio *Georgie Boy* in exchange for a big bag of cash. Keith knew that the Don had a lot of 'black' money to play with, spoils of his illegal gambling operations, and he also knew that the Don was a sucker for buying things. And, obviously, the more equipment Keith could sell Don Georgio for his boat, the more money Keith earned.

Keith was in the process of outfitting an identical boat to *Georgie Boy* for a well-known racing car driver, and every time he bought a new toy for the other boat, he would make a point of driving it under Don Georgio's nose, displaying the new gear.

The game-fishing chair was the best in the world and cost around ten grand. It looked like the barber's chair that Albert Anastasia was murdered in. No doubt a good selling point.

When the Don cast his black eye over that heavily chromed work of art, he was entranced.

'What's that thing?' he asked, pointing at the chair. 'Why don't I have one of them?'

'That's a fighting chair, Don Georgio. The best in the world,' Whitehead replied. 'Looks good on that rig, doesn't it? You're mad if you don't put one on *Georgie Boy*. It'll look special. And besides, it'll help you catch more fish.'

The beautiful thing was the Don Georgio never asked the price of anything. All he wanted to do was catch more fish.

'Then you'd better get me one of those things,' he'd say.

A week later Keith paraded past with the latest pair of pronged outrigger poles fitted to the side of the other boat.

'What are those bastards?' said the Don, pointing at the outriggers.

'Aluminium six-prongers,' Whitehead explained. 'You can troll six marlin baits at once. They're guaranteed to catch you fish.'

No one on the boat knew how to rig a marlin bait, let alone troll six at once, but the poles made the boat look great and the boss had to have a pair.

'Get me those poles too, then,' he demanded.

Within a few days the poles were fitted to *Georgie Boy*, and they looked pretty special.

After six months *Georgie Boy* looked like an ocean-going ship's chandlery. Three radios, radar, satellite navigation, quadraphonic stereo . . . the works. Every possible piece of equipment money could buy.

And so, week after week Whitehead would enquire, 'How'd you go today, Don Georgio? Did you catch any fish?'

Don Georgio's reply was standard. He would scowl at Whitehead.

'No fuckin' fish again today,' he would grumble. 'I spend a hundred Gs on the best boat gear with you and I still can't catch the fucking fish. What's gone wrong?'

This went on for months. One Saturday afternoon, as *Georgie Boy* had just been tied up in its pen fresh back from a day's fishing, Whitehead didn't ask how they went; instead, he offered the Don some advice.

'I think I've worked out why you never catch any fish, Don Georgio,' he said.

The Don was in the barber's chair sipping on a champagne flute and sucking on a White Owl cigar. Chiller had just tied the boat off and was about to cut into his first tinny. Stella was hovering, and an assortment of the Don's cronies were lurking about getting drinks and urging among themselves.

They all pricked their ears to listen to the old master.

'What's the first thing you do when you moor up at Long Reef?' he asked. 'In fact, don't even bother answering. I know — you turn all the toys on at once, don't you?'

'Of course I do' the Don replied. 'What's the use of the gear if I'm not going to use it?'

'It's the noise,' replied Whitehead.

'What do you mean, it's the noise?'

'Well, you've got the stereos going at nine million decibels and the generator at full bore to run the airconditioning, right? And you know how Chiller likes to watch the radar beacon going round and round. Then there's the echo sounders, the two-way radios and the Randwick Races.

'And Stella's high heels on the deck don't help. Believe me, Don Georgio. I reckon I've worked out why you don't catch any fish. It's the noise.'

'What do you mean — it's the fuckin' noise?' The Don couldn't understand what Keith was trying to say and was getting the shits.

'Let me explain,' Keith continued. 'All that racket that you make in the boat goes straight through the hull and bounces off the reef, scaring the shit out of the fish. They all piss off. It's as simple as that. It's the noise — that's why you don't catch any fish.'

The Don looked at his motley crew in amazement.

'Well, I'll be!' he exclaimed. 'So that's what's been goin' wrong.

You smart-arse bastard. Why didn't some other smart bastard tell me that? You are one very clever fella you know that?'

Whitehead kept a straight face.

With that the Don got up from his barber's chair and walked over to the coffin-sized Esky at the back of the boat. He opened the lid. It was chock-a-block with giant snapper. Whitehead's eyes nearly fell out of his head.

'OK, Mr Boat Dealer, you're so smart' Don Georgio said, holding up two whoppers. 'Now I suppose you're going to tell me that these fuckin' beauties are all deaf.'

The crew cracked up.

You see, unbeknown to Keith, Don Georgio had recruited the services of the legendary Sydney Harbour boatman-cum-fisherman, Dicey Frankman and on Dicey's directions and knowledge of the moon, tides and the currents, they had filled the boat with fish. Even Stella, Chiller and all of the urgers got to catch a fish. The Don was hooked and from that day on he lived for fishing. And Dicey knew where to find 'em.

He showered Dicey with gifts and told him that if he ever fished with anyone else he'd have the poor bastard's boat blown out of the water and he'd piss down the owner's throat after he'd slit it.

And yes, Dicey had heard *that* particular story and saw to it that he was available whenever the Don needed him to take him fishing.

But when Dicey got horribly pissed one night and fell off the end of the Double Bay marina and the cops found him two days later in Rose Bay covered in prawns and very deceased, the Don was distraught.

'You think I'm gunna rub out the guy who catches me all the fish?' he explained to the cops who, naturally enough, considered him a prime murder suspect.

But we all knew it was an accident. The Don loved Dicey and the fact was that without him he couldn't catch any fish and this proved to be the truth.

And, try as he may, Don Georgio couldn't get anyone else to fish with him and put him on all the top spots and rig the baits. It seemed as though the whole waterfront had heard the stories about the Don's unusual urinary habits.

With no one to find him the fish, Don Georgio eventually gave up fishing and, as the newly introduced TAB started to take a giant slice out of his illegal gambling, he ventured further into sinister activities.

Often we would see the magnificent *Georgie Boy* moored up in some secluded bay on Sydney Harbour with a bunch of bad-looking dudes on board. Now Keith gave Don Georgio a giant body swerve because he said he was mixed up in heavy drugs these days and that it was only a matter of time before something went wrong.

And it did. One day Don Georgio disappeared off the face of the planet.

But we figured that his love of fishing wasn't all in vain.

According to Mob folklore, Don Georgio sleeps with the fishes.

The Darker Side of Fishing Knives

Believe it or not, the humble fishing knife has many places in history but, sadly, the more notorious of these incidents had little or nothing whatever to do with fishing. A sharp fishing knife is a lethal weapon indeed. But a blunt one can be even more deadly in the wrong hands.

It would be fair comment to say that more accidents are caused by fishing knives than any other 10 fishing implements combined (discounting the odd fishhook in the flesh, that is). Fishing knives have also played many roles in history, but certainly not those of cutting up fish or fishing line.

In 1961, a slightly built inoffensive-looking young man walked into Mick Simmons Sports Store in Sydney's Haymarket and purchased a fishing knife, explaining to the sales assistant that he was going to try his luck around Sydney Harbour.

It's a pity that the young man didn't tell the sales assistant what he was going to try his luck at . . . it could have saved a few lives. You see, his specialty was stabbing derelicts (dozens of times) to death and then removing their private parts with his razor-sharp fishing knife.

When bodies started turning up all over Sydney with their crown jewels missing, the killer became known as 'The Mutilator' and Sydney was under lock and key every night.

And in typical Australian tradition, these ghastly murders started a spate of Mutilator jokes:

'They sighted The Mutilator at Sydney Airport this morning.'

'Really. What was he doing there?'

'Looking for Ansett's hangars.'

And when a murdered derelict's private parts were found in Sydney Harbour, not far from the murder scene, it was the laugh of the day that they were found by 'foreskin divers'.

And in what was to become one of the most famous newspaper headlines in Australian history, *The Case Of The Walking Corpse*, The Mutilator was eventually caught, in bizarre circumstances — a man almost collapsed with shock when he recognised, and had a conversation with, an ex-workmate in George Street, Sydney, a man whose funeral he had attended only months earlier.

He had just spoken to a walking dead man, and he reported it immediately to the police.

The police acted swiftly and apprehended the man. They then found out that the badly decomposed remains of a male person found at a Sydney shop and buried as that of the shop's proprietor, William McDonald, were not McDonald. He had fled Sydney after murdering the man, another derelict, by inflicting multiple stab wounds upon him with his fishing knife.

Months later McDonald returned to Sydney, unaware that the other man had been buried in his name and that he had committed the perfect crime.

Had McDonald stayed interstate or not been sighted by the ex-workmate, the Mutilator murders could quite possibly have remained unsolved, though experts believe that The Mutilator and his razor-sharp fishing knife would have continued on their killing spree until they were eventually caught.

William 'The Mutilator' McDonald was found guilty of multiple murders, and committed to an institution for the criminally insane, where he remains even now, well away, we hope, from the kitchen, and the knife section.

How's that for a charming little fishing knife story?

And I suppose we can only wonder if Mick 'Crocodile' Dundee would have roamed off into the sunset with his beautiful young New York lady reporter friend if it hadn't been for the fishing knife that he plunged into the noggin of the giant croc that almost ate her as she bathed beside the billabong in that skimpy costume (which no red-blooded Aussie boy will ever forget).

What's that? It wasn't a fishing knife? I'm sorry to have to tell you this, but . . . Yes, it was. *We* all know that Mick used it for skinning crocs, but as killing crocs and removing their valuable skin was illegal, he conveniently called it his 'fishing' knife and the authorities were none the wiser.

And if the writers of *Crocodile Dundee* had written the truth, it would have changed one of the great movie lines of all time. It would have gone like this: 'That's not a fishing knife. *This* is a fishing knife.' No way, that sounds terrible. Thank God they didn't. It's much better the way it is.

And then there's the tragic incident a couple of years ago when a young man was minding his own business fishing for bream on Sydney's Coogee Beach.

A young teacher was conducting a high school excursion nearby when a couple of the schoolboys snuck off and allegedly went through the fisherman's bag, removing several articles, including his car keys.

An altercation followed, resulting in the death of the teacher, from a single stab wound to the chest from the man's fishing knife. The young fisherman was eventually tried, convicted of manslaughter and sent to prison.

Fishing knives are among the most lethal legal implements ever invented, and I've lost count of the number of accidents that I'm aware of caused by them on a boat or in the normal course of a day's fishing.

You see, there are no legal requirements or regulations controlling fishing knives, simply because it would be impossible to enforce them. It's stupid to even contemplate regulating fishing knives; the only sensible approach is to educate folks on how to avoid coming to grief with one.

Blind Freddy will tell you that fishing knives come in all shapes and sizes and that most tackle boxes and boats carry at least a couple, the most popular being the general purpose model with a thick blade, a blade guard and a scaler on the back, the other being the filleting knife, vital for cleaning your catch on the spot and taking home the fillets.

The two best tips I can give you on fishing knives are that they should be kept in the sheaf or similar safety cover at all times, and that they must be kept sharp.

A blunt knife is five times more dangerous than a sharp one. Why? With a blunt knife you try a lot harder. If you are filleting a fish and the knife isn't sharp and is cutting roughly, you tend to lean on it a little bit more. Chances are you'll end up with it in some part of your body, particularly if you do it the way most people do, with the blade going toward yourself.

Blunt knives tend to get rusty more quickly, and if they do happen to inflict a wound on someone, the chances of that person catching some horrible disease, such as tetanus, are high.

Just try to imagine the beautiful little germ traps on a fishing knife encrusted with rust and muck. Then try and imagine it going into your flesh. Yuk. So keep it clean, sharp and rust free. And always remember to fillet *away* from your body.

Also remember that the fish you intend to take home for dinner deserve to die with dignity, and a razor-sharp knife will see to it that their throats are cut swiftly and cleanly, with the minimum amount of cruelty.

On boats over the years I've seen people sit on fishing knives, fall on them, grab the blades, slice their fingers off with them and accidentally stab themselves and others with them.

The smartest move you'll ever make is to see to it that your fishing knives are in their sheaths at all times, instead of lying around on the rocks or baitboard on the boat.

Remember that all fishing knives have points — very, very pointed points, designed to penetrate tough skin and bone. They are meant to cut through skulls and tails and scales and fins and beaks, so just about any part of the human anatomy is a piece of cake for a fishing knife.

If you can use one, a butcher's steel is perfect for keeping a fine edge on the blade. Sharpen the knife on a stone and then just tickle it sharp with the butcher's steel when it looks and feels as though it's going blunt.

Files are useless for on-the-spot sharpening and the sharpening stone should be kept in the workshop at home simply because it takes forever to sharpen a knife on one, particularly at sea. Remember what you're out there for . . . to fish, not sharpen knives; that's a home job.

After a series of nasty accidents involving knives on a boat I crewed on for a couple of seasons a few years back, we all went and brought one of those multi-purpose pocketknives.

I'm sure you know the ones I mean. They are like a Swiss Army knife but without all the gadgets. They just have things that are applicable to fishing — fold-up blades, scissors, wire cutters, pliers — and they retail for about $80 to $100.

Each one of us carried one of these for cutting wire, nylon and all the dozens of other little things you need a fishing knife for. When we needed to fillet a fish or cut through bone or skin on a big fish, we'd get out the knife designed specifically for that purpose. No more accidents.

Oh, one last thing. If your big fishing knife was in your belt rather than in your tackle box, you'd be charged for carrying a lethal weapon. Because outside of what fishing knives were designed for, that's exactly what they are.

Mugged in Paradise

Of all of the mighty fish in the world's oceans, few are more colourful and spectacular than the Pacific sailfish. And they don't come much bigger and wilder than the ones that wreak havoc in the waters off Hamilton Island on the Great Barrier Reef. Sailfish hunt in packs and leap high in the air when hooked. If they were humans, they would be hoodlums of the worst possible kind.

It was like driving down the darkest alley in New York and knowing that sooner or later something dreadful was going to happen. But we weren't in New York, we were on a boat at sea and it was broad daylight.

And my premonition wasn't wrong. Just as we circled a flock of birds working a school of bait fish on the surface, there they were — a gang of hoodlums intent on demolishing everything that we were trolling off the back of the boat: baits, lures and teasers.

Nothing was safe from this colourful gang of ocean-going thugs . . . thugs that anglers travel the world in search of.

In a split second they were on us. Mayhem.

Every rod buckled and every reel groaned, as we were mugged by a gang of notoriously tough aquatic gangsters — the legendary whopper Hamilton Island sailfish.

Our crew of skipper Aussie Tauranac, Peter Kidd, Peter Street and myself were fishing the annual Hamilton Island Billfish Bonanza aboard Aussie's superb 16-metre game-boat *Capricorn.* It was our second day out.

Day one we pulled the wrong rein and went south of Hamilton in search of the elusive sailfish. Nothing. The bite was up north of nearby Hayman Island.

A GANG OF
NO~BUT
AN' WE'LL

BAD SAILFISH? COME ALONGSIDE COMPARE NOTES...
STAY LOW
DEY GOT REEBOKS?

And up north they were snappin' their heads off. Every boat that had elected to fish that area the day before had caught fish. Some had two, three and even four hooked up at once.

Next morning we were there at sparrowfart for a copybook start and we had tagged and released a nice little sail of around 40 kilograms by 10am. I had a combination of garfish baits, lures and a teaser trolling over the back and the sail had come up and had a good look at all of them before moving from one to the other and driving us nuts for about 10 minutes as we tried to coax it into biting.

In the end the little sail got hopping mad and I fed him a freshly-rigged wolf herring bait which it gutsed down. It jumped all over the ocean and performed beautifully at the side of the boat as we tagged it and sent it back to its mother. The camera crew we had on board were ecstatic. Great footage for so early in the day.

By midday we were in the thick of the action — but no more bites. In a six kilometre radius there were 16 game-boats trolling baits and lures for sailfish. We had fish jumping all around us, but we couldn't turn a reel! Boy, were we frustrated.

Sailfish were free jumping all over the place and as many as four boats at a time were hooked up within visual range. The place was crawling with fish but my variety of cunningly rigged enticements remained untouched.

We had a few lookers come up and inspect what we had on offer but they just wouldn't go on with it. We were disappointed, to say the least. I rigged and rerigged the baits and changed the lures for ones with brighter colours, trying every trick in the book.

At 3pm every boat around us was playing a fish. This was the hottest spot of the day. A concentration of sailfish that sent scouting parties out to maraud . . . or so it seemed.

And so we trolled through the mayhem. Something had to happen . . . and it did. We got mugged.

I'm not sure how many there were, probably 10 of them and all around 60 kilograms, certainly formidable opponents on the eight kilogram breaking-strain line we were using.

In the swish of a tail they were on us. Gangs of sails don't muck around. A sailfish knows that if it doesn't get in first, then there's another waiting in line that will.

The first one came up and smashed the bright-pink lure trolled in the wake of the boat. Before Peter had time to grab the rod, another pulverised a garfish bait trolled through the left outrigger and took off for New Zealand.

In the instant that it took for all this to happen another three had demolished the three remaining baits.

To add to the confusion, four more were attacking the huge hookless teaser we had hanging off the back and attached to 450 kilogram breaking-strain sash cord.

I had never seen anything like it. We all had fish on at once, jumping all over the ocean in different directions.

One line crossed another — instant bust-up. One gone. One threw the hook. Two down.

The light wire on the double-hook-rigged garfish gave out. Three away.

There was just mine left — about 60 kilograms of hopping mad sailfish jumping around the boat. Just when it looked like I was solidly hooked up, one of its mates picked up the teaser hanging in the wake and stretched the sash cord to breaking point just as the fish ran my line over it. Gone.

And then there was nothing. It was all over in two minutes. They left us with smashed gear and reputations. Even an old fisho like me had trouble coming to terms with what had just happened.

Our crew was in a state of shock. Speechless. In 120 seconds that gang of finned hitmen had destroyed us and moved on.

Then we heard yelling and screaming coming from a boat a couple of hundred metres away. They had half-a-dozen fish on at once and within a couple of minutes they also had nothing left. No doubt the same gang.

Thank Christ none of us were wearing Reeboks or Nikes — the bastards would have jumped into the boat and like their street gang counterparts on dry land, mugged us for our shoes.

The Shark Arm Murder

What started out as a day's fishing ended up as one of the most bizarre murder mysteries the world has known. Straight out of an Agatha Christie novel, this extraordinary true story had the lot. A giant shark, human body parts, shadowy suspects and another grisly murder.

Operators of Sydney's Coogee Aquarium, father and son Bert and Ron Hobson, couldn't believe their good fortune. They had had a very successful morning's fishing on 18 April 1935, with a captured two-metre shark ready to be taken back to their exhibition, when a monster tiger shark cruised up, ate the smaller shark and became entangled in their net.

What a catch! The bigger shark would prove to be a valuable attraction, much more so than the smaller fish. But from the outset, when released into the aquarium, the huge fish appeared to be 'off-colour' and disoriented.

On Anzac Day, when a crowd had gathered at the aquarium to view the latest exhibition, it suddenly shuddered and regurgitated the remains of a human arm, much to the horror of the onlookers. The police were called immediately.

Close examination by police revealed that the arm carried a tattoo of two boxers 'shaping up' and also had a length of rope tied around the wrist. Puzzled as to why the shark would vomit up the arm, authorities concluded that under normal circumstances the big shark would have digested it, but it was obviously feeling a bit ill, no doubt due to its new surroundings.

The shark was put out of its misery five days later.

A post-mortem examination of the shark's stomach contents revealed nothing else and it was concluded that it was the smaller shark which the tiger had eaten that had swallowed the arm in the first place.

But they didn't need the shark alive to arrive at their more grisly conclusion; the arm had not been bitten off. Oh no! It was the work of a knife or a scalpel in the hands of a very inept surgeon.

An anatomy student perhaps . . . but that line of investigation was eliminated by two big slashes near the laceration, indicating extreme violence.

It seemed the body had been cut into bits and thrown into the sea to be eaten by the fish and remain forever just another unsolved 'missing persons' case. Who would have ever guessed that a shark would have brought up the evidence in an aquarium?

One can only wonder what the murderer must have thought when the story hit the headlines. What rotten luck!

The theories came thick and fast. One was that perhaps the arm had been preserved in formalin or some other kind of embalming fluid in a hospital for students to study. This theory was soon discounted when it was established that the arm had only been in the water a matter of days.

Yet another of the more plausible theories put forward was that it was the arm of an escaped mental patient whose body was found floating in Sydney Harbour . . . minus an arm. That story turned out to be a hoax.

But there was no escaping the fact that Sydney had been the scene of a murder most foul.

And while the scientists were trying to put the pieces together, so to speak, a man identified the arm through photographs in the paper to be that of his brother, 40-year-old James Smith, a Sydney billiards saloon marker, SP bookmaker and ex-employee of Sydney boat-builder, Reginald Holmes.

In the meantime, a well-known 42-year-old Sydney criminal and close associate of James Smith, a certain John Patrick Brady, was charged with the murder of Smith. The case was built on the fact that he had recently visited the Sydney home of Reginald Holmes, who had had recent unsatisfactory business dealings with Smith.

Police instigated a mammoth search around the Cronulla and Port Hacking districts, as Brady had recently moved from a cottage in the area, taking with him a tin storage trunk, an anchor and two heavy window weights.

On 19 May, *The Truth* newspaper reported: 'Operating on the theory that the body might have been carved up, and perhaps only the arm with the identifying tattoo had been consigned to the waves, the police dug up certain premises, dragged the bottom of the bay, searched the tide-washed rocks, scoured the sandhills, but to no avail. The mystery is still as deep, and as apparently unsolvable as ever.'

Brady denied any involvement in the murder of Smith and in his statement to police said that he had last seen the dead man with Holmes and another man.

Shortly after the police began a search for the elusive boatbuilder, a bizarre twist in the story took place. On the evening of 21 May, Sydney Water Police pursued a launch that was reported to be behaving in an erratic and dangerous fashion on Sydney Harbour.

During the ensuing four-hour chase, the wayward vessel attempted to ram the police launch four times before being apprehended. The driver turned out to be Reginald Holmes, dazed, and with blood pouring from a gunshot wound to his head.

While he claimed to have been fired upon and that he believed the police to be his clandestine attackers, police took possession of a .32 pistol, believing that the unstable Holmes had attempted to kill himself but the shot had only grazed his head.

Holmes told detectives that Brady had murdered Smith and dumped his body, in a trunk, off Port Hacking and had threatened Holmes' life if he 'dobbed' him in.

No charges were laid against Holmes and he was allowed to leave having promised to reveal this valuable information at an inquest into the death of James Smith.

But Reginald Holmes never made it to the inquest. On 11 June, Holmes was found slumped over the steering wheel of his car, parked near the Sydney Harbour Bridge, with three bullets to the head. He had been shot at close range with a .32 calibre pistol.

Patrick Brady was in police custody charged with the murder of Smith at the time of Holmes' murder.

At the inquest, the surprise witness turned out to be the wife of the recently deceased Holmes, Mrs Inie Parker-Holmes. She revealed her late husband's business dealings with Brady. Her husband had told her how Brady had confessed to killing Smith and placing the cut-up body in a trunk and dumping it at sea.

A real estate agent, P.H. Forbes, pointed out Brady as the person who had rented a cottage from him under the name of 'Mr Williams'. This person had later vacated the cottage, taking with him various items, including a tin trunk which had been replaced by a larger new one.

Patrick Brady was committed for trial for the murder of James Smith.

But the case was still shrouded in mystery. Persistent rumours of underworld conspiracies, narcotics trafficking and gangsters dogged the trial, which was held in front of Mr Justice Jordan at the Central Criminal Court.

Brady admitted that on the night of 8 April, he had accompanied Smith back to his cottage but steadfastly maintained that Smith had left in the company of well-known Sydney waterfront identities Albert Stannard and John Patrick Strong.

Brady was eventually acquitted because of insufficient evidence. He changed his name and dropped out of sight completely.

Stannard and Strong were charged with the murder of Holmes, tried twice and also eventually acquitted.

And like all cases where fact makes fiction look ridiculous, there was one last twist to the tale. On October 30, 1952, a fire at the Holmes residence took the life of Mrs Inie Parker-Holmes, eliminating the last link with the infamous Shark Arm Murder.

Fangs for the Memories

For a fish living in warm waters anywhere in the world, one of the prime requisites is to have long, sharp teeth — and plenty of 'em. There are the hunters and the hunted, and contrary to popular belief, not all fish have teeth. The ones without 'em certainly got the rough end of the stick!

One of the great fallacies about fishing is that all fish have teeth. Not so. In fact I'd go so far as to say that there would be as many gummy fish out there as there are fish with choppers. Mind you, in that world below the waves, where the one with the longest or sharpest teeth wins, if I had to live down there, I'd rather be crockeried-up than not.

Believe it or not, kingfish, marlin, most tunas, sailfish, trevally, trout and garfish don't have teeth at all. But coral trout, bream, snapper and barracouta do. Mullet don't need them because they were put on this planet to be eaten by toothy critters, not to do the eating.

Tailor are most certainly fanged, and their nickname of 'choppers' comes from their ability to chop the tails off their prey with their teeth, rendering them helpless. Then it's pounce, then eat.

But tailor themselves are much sought after by predators such as jewfish, kingfish, tuna and salmon, and when there's a school of tailor getting into the bait fish, you can bet your life that there's a bunch of bigger predators waiting in the wings to get stuck into the tailor.

Bream use their teeth and jaws to crack open oysters, mussels and crustaceans. Snapper use that big bump on their noggins to bash oysters and other morsels from reefs, then they munch on them with their molars to get at the succulent meat inside.

Only a couple of common tunas have teeth: the bonito and a horrifying gangster of a thing called the dogtooth tuna. The dogtooth is so appropriately named, because its mouth is a dentist's nightmare and each one of the dental daggers has a point that could chew the chrome off a tow bar.

Combine this with the dogtooth's ravenous appetite and determination to escape when hooked, and you've got one of the most formidable critters ever to swim the warm oceans of the world. I regard the dogtooth as one of the greatest fighting fish of our warmer northern waters.

Bait fish such as pilchards, yellowtail, slimy mackerel and whitebait don't have teeth because, like the mullet, they were put here by Mother Nature to be eaten, not to do the eating.

On the other hand, a couple of horrendous biters that can be found on and around the Great Barrier Reef and northern Australia, the wahoo and the Spanish mackerel, were designed to bite and kill anything that is stupid enough to swim within biting range. Of all the killing machines in the ocean, this pair would have to take out the 'daily double' in speed and killing efficiency.

Wahoo and Spanish mackerel are long torpedo-shaped fish that can travel at amazing speed, especially when they are coming in for the kill. With triangle-shaped mouths and an assortment of vampire's teeth that could bite through a broomstick, they prey on their unsuspecting neighbours with lightning speed.

Up north they call the mixture of the wahoo, Spanish mackerel and the assortment of other mackerels (including the spotted and the scaly mackerels) that hang out with them 'the razor gang', because they have the uncanny ability to be able to cut a whole swimming fish bait in half without ever getting hooked on the hook's barb, which is secreted in the bait's belly, usually about an eighth of an inch in front of the bite.

Off Sydney in the 1970s we caught a 20 kilogram wahoo (which was extremely unusual this far south), whacked it with the donger and put it in the icebox to fillet later and have for dinner — they are as good to eat as they are to catch.

One of our woman crew members lifted the fish out of the box later and, as she did so, she accidentally ran its gaping mouth over another woman crew member's leg, cutting the skin to the bone and causing her to be hospitalised and have about 20 stitches. That's how sharp a wahoo's teeth are. They can still get you long after they're dead.

Barramundi don't have teeth, not that they really need 'em anyway because they wolf down their prey without chewing on them first.

There are so many dangerous characters lurking about in the ocean, particularly in northern Australia, that it looks more like the remand yard at Pentridge than a fish paradise. Everything that lives there is out to chew the butt off everything else.

These warm waters are also the haunt of another horrifically toothed denizen — the barracuda. The only fish that has been known to attack human beings, time and time again, especially divers.

Unlike the wahoo and the mackerel, the barracuda (not to be confused with the southern barracouta) has protruding, gripping (rather than biting) front teeth that would make a bull terrier's fangs look like a couple of carpet tacks.

And as the nasty old barracuda gets bigger, so do his Jack Langs. By the time he's a couple of metres long, his two front choppers look like a pair of concrete nails and could put holes in a baseball bat.

When it gets to this size, the barracuda becomes known as a 'great barracuda' ('great' as in big, that is, not as in 'fun guy', because they would be about the unfunniest thing that swims) and, in their old age, great barracuda become extremely territorial; most reefs have a barracuda as their prime predator. Sort of like the local bad guy.

While lots of divers have been bitten, or at least attacked, experts believe that it is not because the great barracuda likes taking chunks out of humans. Rather, they believe that because barracuda usually hang out and attack in murky water, poor visibility means the 'cuda confuses the diver for a fish they would like to eat.

Southern Australian whiting have small teeth for chomping open pippies and other crustaceans they find while fossicking along the bottom.

Flathead also have small, yet effectively sharp fangs for munching on their favourite tucker — small, live baitfish.

So next time you catch a fish, no matter what species, have a look at the crockery department before you let it go. You might be surprised at what you'll find.

Fishing's Urban Myths

Being the pastime that it is, fishing is susceptible to more exaggerations and outright lies than all the other recreational activities combined. And I've heard them all at one stage or another. The most frightening part of it is that the tellers of these exaggerated out-of-all-proportion whoppers usually try and convince me they were there when it happened, putting the story into the 'urban myth' category. Like, give me a break . . .

An urban myth is a preposterous story told and re-told so many times that the tellers not only end up believing it themselves, but they try to convince anyone silly enough to listen that they were actually there when it happened.

Or that their uncle, aunt, wife's brother or whoever told them was there when it happened. You must have heard an urban myth. Like the woman who never washed her beehive hairdo and ended up with a nest of spiders living in it.

Or the woman who took her beloved French poodle into the Chinese restaurant and asked the staff to look after it while she had dinner. Only after the lady and her friends had finished their banquet and she went to collect Fifi, did they find out that the dog was one of the exotic dishes.

And then there's the one about the bloke who was kissing and cuddling his girl at the drive-in when a gang of hoodlums picked up the back of his car and started bouncing it up and down. Starting the engine, he planted his foot to the floor and the next time the wheels hit the ground he took off at a million miles an hour. When he got home he found a human arm, dripping blood, caught up in the bumper bar.

Anyone who would believe that crap would believe that Elvis was Jewish. But I can still see some readers saying: 'Dad, Paul B. Kidd reckons that that story you told us about Auntie Joan's first cousin's sister's boyfriend's next-door neighbour's dog gettin' eaten in the Chinese restaurant is a load of crap.'

'Well, he don't know what he's talkin' about, son, because I was there and if I hadn't seen it with my own eyes, I wouldn't have believed it, either.'

But he wasn't there and he didn't see it because it didn't happen. It's all bullshit. It's an urban myth.

The trouble is, urban myths seem to badly afflict the fishing fraternity, too. Must be something to do with all the practice they get talking about the one that got away.

One such story is about a group of Tasmanians who went to Melbourne for a national fishing club convention. So familiar were these blokes with all the old jokes they regularly told each other that rather than repeat the details of the joke time and again, they had given them all numbers and would go into fits of laughter every time someone got up onto a chair and yelled 'Number 27', 'Number 23', and so on.

Told what was going on, the Melbourne club president couldn't believe it, so one of the Tasmanians invited him to have a go. Feeling like a fool, he stood on the chair and yelled 'Number 66'.

The Tasmanians fell about, laughing even harder than before. 'That brought the house down, didn't it!' the president said to the Tasmanian.

'Why wouldn't it?' he replied. 'We haven't heard it before.'

The fifty blokes I know who swear blind that they were there that night and heard it, are having themselves on. It didn't happen. It's an urban myth.

Neither did the one about the bloke who sought revenge on one of the meanest critters that swims and wound up in the worst possible way.

It's no secret that the huge kingfish that live in the caves that honeycomb the cliffs that disappear into the deep water at Jervis Bay, on the NSW south coast, are a bunch of pests.

HEARD
IT...

NUMBER
FORTY
SIX

They duck out of their caves and grab the rockhoppers' catches as they are about to lift them from the water. Then it's straight back into the cave and goodnight to the anglers' catch and gear.

Our hero had lost hundreds of fish to them over the years and figured that if he could hook one of these monsters on heavy enough gear and hang on, then one of two things could happen; the line would break or he would catch the fish and teach it a lesson. So he bought a mammoth game-fishing reel and filled it up with 500 pound breaking-strain line. Then he strapped a huge game-fishing rod to himself with a harness that would normally be used for catching tiger sharks.

And so he could hang on when the monster struck, he positioned himself in a chair-like structure among the rocks, bracing his feet against two large boulders about 20 metres from the rock face that disappeared into kingfish alley.

Then he got his mate to drop a live trevally on a 1000 pound trace into the water, pushed the drag on the reel up to beyond breaking point and hung on for grim death as the world's biggest kingfish shouldered about 50 of his mates out of the way, grabbed the trevally and headed back to his cave.

Until then, the theory was working just fine. But when the fish didn't give in and the line didn't break, things went drastically wrong. As the slack took up and the kingie headed to his lounge room with his prize, Boofhead was launched like a Patriot missile out of his rocky fighting chair and dragged screaming on his face, elbows and knees across the rocks to the cliff edge where he, rod, reel and harness disappeared like an Olympic high diver off the cliff and into the sea.

All that remained to prove to the police that the carnage ever took place was some teeth, skin, a shoe, a broken reel handle and a bloodied patch between the rocks. And search as they may, police divers found nothing.

True story? Absolutely, if you choose to believe at least four blokes I know who will swear blind that they were there when it happened. But they didn't see it because it didn't happen. It's all bullshit. But they've told the story so many times that they believe that it actually happened.

It's a fantasy . . . an urban myth.

And then there's the classic of all time. Everyone's heard this little beauty.

The Right Reverend Billy Nile had never been fishing before in his life, so when he caught a 20 kilogram jewfish, his first-ever fish of any description, on a fishing outing on Sydney's Hawkesbury River with the over 60s Born Again Christian Fishing Club, he thought it was a gift from above.

One can only try and imagine what a drab day's fishing it would be out with that lot of god-fearing wowsers. No bad language, no grog; only tea and lots of 'hallelujah brothers' and 'praise the Lord'.

When the Reverend Billy turned up at home that night with the giant fish slung over his shoulder, Mrs Agnes Nile was beside herself with excitement and very proud of her husband's feat.

The following day she rang him at his office. 'Reverend,' she said, 'I have a special surprise for you when you come home tonight. I'll be waiting for you at the front door and I'm going to blindfold you and sit you down and then take off the blindfold and show you what the surprise is.'

He couldn't wait. He half-suspected that it would be a fabulous fish dinner and sure enough, as he drove up the driveway to his home, he copped the stunning aroma of freshly cooked fish. Once inside, he went along with the charade and let his wife blindfold him and lead him into the dining room and sit him down.

'Just be patient,' she purred. 'I'll be back with the surprise in about five minutes. No peeking now.'

Mrs Nile had only been gone about a minute when the Reverend felt this giant fart coming on. It was a ripper. 'Probably those curried egg sandwiches I had for lunch,' he thought.

He held off from letting it go for fear that Mrs Nile would come back in the room and catch him and spend the rest of the night praying for his soul. But when it came on again, so bad that his stomach ached, he had to let it go.

'How long now darling?' he called to the kitchen.

'Only a couple more minutes,' she called back.

Satisfied that he was safe, the Reverend tilted his bum to just the right angle for maximum relief and let out the longest and loudest fart in a long and illustrious sneaky fart career. It was a ripper, and he chuckled to himself at the naughtiness of it all.

And it was off . . . the aroma was putrid, vile, sickening. 'I need pulling through with a knotted blanket,' he chuckled out loud to himself as he waved blindly in the air, laughing his head off and desperately trying to disperse the stench before Mrs Nile returned with the surprise.

A few minutes later she entered the room and told him to take off the blindfold and have a look at his surprise. It was as he had guessed, the whole baked jewfish, done in vegetables and ginger with slices of lemon all along the top.

But that wasn't the only surprise. Seated stony-faced at the huge dining table were the most prominent members of his congregation: the Lord and Lady Mayoress, the local headmistress, the ladies from the Bible Society, the police chief and his wife and assorted wowsers of all descriptions, waiting in silence to surprise him and congratulate him on his catch and share it with him.

Yes, it was a real surprise. So much so that the Right Reverend Billy Nile passed out from the shock of it all and applied for another posting the next day.

Another true story? Absolutely. How do I know? Because I was there.

Now that's got you thinking, hasn't it?

Those Magnificently Mad Makos

Of all of the critters that swim there is nothing more dangerous or maniacal than the mako shark. If they were humans they would spend their entire lives in mental institutions. Everything you read about them is true. I doubt that anyone could have a vivid enough imagination to make anything up about them.

When a three metre, 200 kilogram mako shark tried to eat Gordon Dunlop's 6-metre fibreglass fishing boat about 10 kilometres off Sydney and then attempted to jump into it, it was yet another chapter in a long, long series of incidents involving mako sharks that, if ever written, would be as long as the list of the Liberal Party's broken election promises.

But all of you once-a-year anglers out there needn't worry. The chances of you ever getting bitten, let alone eaten by one, are pretty remote unless you venture out into the very deep waters where the mako, aka the blue pointer, rules the currents and fears absolutely nothing — except, perhaps, bigger and crazier makos.

In fact, if a mako did eat you, your death would not be in vain, as you would go down in history as the first recorded victim of a mako shark in Australian waters. Except, of course, for the folks who may have been frightened to death by them or come very close. And there's no shortage of them. Gordon is now on the end of a very long list.

Yes, makos are homicidal maniacs. Growing to 700 kilograms, and built like a guided missile, with a magnificent steely, silver-blue back with a snow-white undercarriage and eyes as black as a mother-in-

POLICE
SHARK ALLEY

law's curse that follow your every move from the water, the mako shark is Mother Nature's ultimate killing machine.

But man-eaters? No. Certainly not to my knowledge anyway. But the curator of the Taronga Zoo Aquarium, John West (no, I'm not having you on), who also records shark attacks in Australian waters, says differently.

'The mako, a close cousin of the great white shark, is a known man-killer in some parts of the world, but there have been no confirmed attacks in Australia,' John said in an interview. 'But shark experts rate them as *potentially* dangerous.'

Potentially dangerous? That would have to be the greatest understatement since Greg Norman gave up surfing and said, 'I might take up golf. I think I could be good at it.' Potentially dangerous? Really? A shark that has been known to jump into boats and terrorise the living daylights out of the occupants and then jump out again is potentially dangerous?

A shark that on dozens of occasions has been known to grab the propeller or leg of an outboard motor in its crockery-encrusted gob-hole and then shake the motor and boat while the poor wretches on board go white with fear in a real-life scene that would make *Jaws* look like *Here's Humphrey*.

No, makos aren't potentially dangerous . . . they are definitely dangerous. I've been telling stories about the antics of mako sharks for nigh on 30 years now, and I'll tell more about them in a minute, but first let me quote a couple of paragraphs from Gordon's first-hand experience with that horrible critter he encountered while he was berleying and drifting for yellowfin tuna.

'It appeared in the berley and circled the boat before slamming into it a number of times, smashing teeth as it savaged the two outboard motors and part of the gunwale,' Gordon said. 'It left giant gouges in the metal of the main 140 horsepower motor. But things really got interesting when it tried to get into the boat. It came in over the stern and got so close to me I could have poked it in the eye.'

Dodging to avoid the snapping jaws, Gordon hit the mako over the head with a heavy length of wood normally used to stun tuna. It eventually slithered back into the water and swam off, 'shaking its head in the air as if it was convulsing'. Eventually it recovered fully and swam away, much to the relief of Gordon and his crew.

John West believes that the mako's aggressive behavior was a response to the pilchards that the fishermen were throwing over the side to attract tuna, some run-off blood from the bait tank and the electromagnetic fields around the outboard motor. The mako is extremely sensitive to these because they resemble ones produced by the heart muscles of potential prey.

Hmmmm. That's all very well, but having nearly been killed by makos on more than one occasion, I have a different theory. The pilchards, blood and electromagnetic field all add up, but what John has omitted to tell us is that during late August, September and October, the mako sharks gather off the east coast of Australia, particularly off Sydney, to mate. That's right, to mate.

Yeah, I know the old gag: 'How do they do it? Very carefully.' But this is no laughing matter, particularly for the makos. There's some pretty cranky old makos out there at this time of the year and, to make it worse, there's not enough lady makos to go round, so to speak, so they get crankier than usual, particularly if they happen to find a mate and someone tries to take her away or, even worse, succeeds in taking her away.

Every year about this time, my old mate Captain Ross Hunter and I go mako shark fishing off Sydney Heads in his magnificent 12-metre charter boat, *Broadbill*. What we see out there is so pathetic that if it weren't so serious (to the sharks) it would be hilarious, which, to us, it is.

Doey-eyed makos are lolling around on the surface, too lovesick to take a bait or care about anything but a bit of lust. And then there are the others, with giant gouges out of them either from the love-making process, which is extremely aggressive, or from fending off the advances of would-be suitors.

And then there are the ones that appear to have missed out altogether. They scurry about all over the joint, really pissed off, ravenously attacking our baits. Once hooked, they jump all over the ocean. Actually, they don't jump, as such; they launch themselves from the water like guided missiles, and reach heights of up to 10 metres or more out of the water.

It is a behaviour unique to the mako, no matter where or what time of the year you hook them, and it is both breathtaking and terrifying to watch. And yes, they have landed in boats. And yes, more times than once, when a mako has landed in a boat, the occupants have been known to jump out.

Like the time in New Zealand a few years back when a whopper mako jumped into a game-fishing boat and a couple of the anglers jumped over the side while another two fled to the saloon of the boat and locked the door while the mako kicked the game chair, rods and reels into the next postcode.

Only after the fish had exhausted itself did the fishermen gingerly emerge from the saloon and club it to death with a fire extinguisher and help their mates back on board. Is it any wonder that they are referred to in fishing circles as 'blue dynamite with a short fuse'?

Another landed on the deck of a yacht participating in the Sydney to Hobart yacht race once. But the classic story of them all happened off Sydney Heads back in the '70s. A lone angler in his 12-metre cabin cruiser was moored up fishing for snapper on the bottom and sharks on the surface, with a floating bait. The shark bait went off and as he picked up the rod and reel and set the hook, he was amazed to see a huge mako shark, around 350 kilograms, jump clear of the water and land on his line and break it.

Terrified by the size of the mako and aware that he would have no chance of catching it by himself, he put the shark gear away and concentrated on his snapper fishing. But the mako had other ideas. It charged the tuck of the boat a couple of times before making a giant leap, propelling itself into the cockpit where it went berserk and smashed and bit everything in sight.

Our hero fled to the flying bridge where he produced an old .303 rifle and blazed away at the beast that had reduced his beautiful boat to a splintered, blood and foam-soaked mess. But, unfortunately for him, every shot missed the shark and instead went straight through the deck and into the engines or through the bottom of the boat.

The mako jumped over the side and circled the boat as the angler managed to get one engine going, cut the anchor rope and headed for home, with water pouring in from everywhere. In answer to his 'mayday' call, the water police met him halfway and towed him back through the Heads. Only then did the mako stop following the boat and head back out to sea.

And that's a true story. They tell me that ever since that day, the poor bastard won't even drink water with his scotch, let alone go back out fishing in it.

Toady's Revenge

This story is the reason for my belief that if you are cruel to animals, or, for that matter, any living thing, it will come back on you one day. I would ask that all parents encourage their children to read this story to make them aware of the dangers that lie ahead for children who are cruel to harmless animals.

When I was a kid growing up in Perth, my mates and I tried to commit genocide on a loathsome creature called the 'blowie'. Not the blowfly — the blowfish. That's what we called them over there. No matter where we fished, sooner or later the blowies would turn up in their millions and take over. And they were not a pretty sight. Growing to about 30 centimetres long, they were brown along the back with a snow-white underbelly that puffed up like a prickly balloon when they were caught. They had big bulging bug eyes like a cane toad and a pair of square teeth that could eat an apple through a tennis racket.

To say the least, they were bloody pests. Once they showed up we had to pack up and leave, because the chance of catching anything else was pretty remote. They were useless for anything. No good as bait and we read regularly in the papers how people had died or at least got very sick from eating them. And so, with the full approval of the Department of Fisheries, we took it upon ourselves to rid Perth's waterways of this menace.

We killed every one that we caught. And savage little bastards that we were, we devised the most horrific methods of dispatch imaginable. We stabbed them, threw them under cars on the Canning Bridge, teed off using them as golf balls, left them to die in agony in the hot sun, extracted their teeth while they were still alive and let them go with their entrails hanging out so the other blowies could eat them alive.

My father was appalled at the carnage. 'Let me tell you a little story about life,' he once said to me as he sat me down and tried to explain to me how whatever we do always comes back to us in some form or another. He called it 'karma'. 'When I was a young boy living on a farm,' he said, 'there was a billy goat living in the paddock next-door. The poor old billy goat had never done anything to me, but I used to chuck rocks at it all the time. I never hit it and it was smart enough to stay out of range. For this reason the grass grew long and rich close to the fence because the billy goat never came close enough to eat it for fear of being hit with a rock.

'So I stayed away for awhile. Sure enough, the goat started to graze closer and closer to the fence, gaining more and more bravado as each day passed. So one day when it was happily munching away just on the other side of the fence, I snuck up and threw a full house brick at it and hit it square between the eyes. The poor old goat went down and didn't move. I was mortified. I had no idea that I would kill it. I just wanted to have some fun with it and now it was stone dead. My father thrashed me to within an inch of my life. And as if that wasn't bad enough, he made a chilling prediction that would live with me to this very day.

'He said that no matter where I went or whatever I did, that goat would haunt me for the rest of my days. It may not be in the shape of a goat; it could be a future boss, a bad motor car or just a bad circumstance in life. But no matter what, every time something rotten happened, I could bet my life that if I closed my eyes tight enough, I'd see that goat looking up at me and laughing its head off.

'And it was true. All my life, whenever something has gone wrong or bad unforeseen circumstances occurred, that goat flashed across my consciousness, and sure enough, when I closed my eyes, there it was, having a laugh at my expense. Mind you, what you are doing to those unfortunate blowies is nowhere near as bad as what I did to that poor old goat, because the blowies are toxic pests, but you can bet your life that somewhere, sometime, there will be an even up. Life's like that.'

I discarded as a load of crap what my wise old dad had told me and went about devising new horrendous methods of disposing of the blowies. We set fire to them, skinned them alive and gouged their eyes out. So much for 'karma'. I told my mates about what Dad had said and they would stab the blowies repeatedly and yell out 'karma, karma, karma' while they were doing it. We were horrid little beasts.

And then in my late teens I moved to Sydney and blowies became a thing of the past — they are very rare around these parts. Soon I had forgotten about them altogether as I pursued a blowie-less fishing career off the stunning rock ledges, undersea mountains and in the warm ocean currents that combine to make the eastern seaboard of Australia one of the fishiest places on Earth. In the late '60s I started writing feature fishing stories for the national magazines and I did a weekly column in the local Sydney eastern suburbs newspaper. In 1972 I opened a fishing tackle shop in Bondi Junction which became the centre of fishing activity in the district. I had set myself up as the local expert, which, in hindsight, left me wide open for any form of practical joke. After all, experts are supposed to be invincible, aren't they?

So when my mate Ray Bourke asked me to partner him in the local fishing Derby, which offered cash prizes for the heaviest of *any* species weighed, I jumped at the chance. Ray was a hot-shot angler and knew Sydney Harbour and the close offshore reefs backwards. If we couldn't take out a few prizes, no one could, and we started red-hot favourites in the event.

But it just wasn't my day. We fished Long Reef about six kilometres off Sydney Heads in Ray's 9-metre boat, and just before daylight Ray caught a jewie that would go about 25 kilograms. As the sun was coming up he boated a nice snapper of around seven kilograms, and by midmorning he'd caught an assortment of reef fish which included nannygai, sergeant baker and morwong. I hadn't had a bite. By lunchtime I was starting to wonder if I had leprosy, but then I had a solid bite and hooked up. It was a heavy fish and it seemed that it was its bulk rather than its fighting ability that kept me busy on the six kilogram line for about 10 minutes.

At last it was alongside the boat and Ray got between me and the fish, which I was yet to see, and netted it. 'Struth, mate,' he yelled.

'What a whopper. It's the biggest toadfish I've ever seen in my life. You'll win a prize with this one for sure.'

Toadfish? What the bloody hell was a toadfish? I was soon to find out as Ray lifted the net and emptied its contents into the bottom of the boat. Oh no!!!! I couldn't believe my eyes. It was the biggest blowie I had ever seen in my life. So that's what they called blowies in the eastern states — toadfish. It must have been 60 centimetres long and weighed about four kilograms. And there it was smiling up at me from the deck with its buck teeth, grunting and puffing and farting as much to say, 'Hello, Paul, haven't you been expecting me?'

No, I hadn't. Yuk! All those memories of the unspeakable things that I had done to his ancestors came flooding back and my father's words were ringing in my ears, 'It's called "karma", son.'

'Good on you, mate,' Bourkie said, 'that'll weigh and you can bet that no one else will catch a toady bigger than that. That's if anyone catches one at all. They're pretty rare around these parts.'

So rare that I'd never heard anyone mention them. 'But I can't weigh a blowie,' I protested.

'Rubbish,' he said. 'The contest says the biggest of *any* species and that's a species. You'll get a good cash prize.'

Despite my protests, he put the vile, grunting and blurting beast into the capture bag with his assortment of reef fish and we headed into the weigh-in at Watsons Bay, where a huge crowd, including press photographers and TV cameramen, had gathered. As Ray and I had started favourites, we got a big cheer as both of us carried the huge bag full of fish to the scales. The onlookers oohed and aahed and cheered and applauded as Ray produced fish after fish that took out the prizes in their field.

'Come on mate, it's your turn now,' Bourkie called to me as there was only the one giant bulge left in the bag. The crowd hummed in anticipation. But their sighs of enthusiasm turned to shrieks of laughter as I up-ended the bag and the giant blowie rolled out. It collected grass cuttings all along its body as it rolled along. When it came to a stop, it looked for all the world like a slimy, green, grinning lamington.

It brought the house down when the weighmaster held the stinking thing up by its tail and the crowd chanted in unison, 'Toady, toady, toady' and all pointed at me. 'Come on, Paul, you should know better than to try to weigh this rotten thing,' the weighmaster said above the laughter, 'they've been outlawed in every State for donkey's years.'

I looked at Bourkie, who had collapsed laughing. I'd been set up beautifully and I had to cop it sweet or be a bad sport. The blowies had had their revenge. It took me a long time to live it down, and I still cringe whenever anyone yells out 'Toady'.

My old dad was right. And let this be a lesson to all of you out there who are cruel to dumb animals. They will always come back to you in some form or another.